The Practice of Loving Kindness

The Practice of **Loving Kindness**

a guide to spiritual fulfillment and social harmony

Vincent Ryan Ruggiero

New City Press

Published in the United States by New City Press
202 Cardinal Rd., Hyde Park, NY 12538
©2003 Vincent Ryan Ruggiero

Cover design by Lucia Colella

Library of Congress Cataloging-in-Publication Data:

Ruggiero, Vincent Ryan.
    The practice of loving kindness : a guide to spiritual fulfillment & social harmony /
Vincent Ryan Ruggiero.
        p. cm.
    ISBN 1-56548-180-1
        1. Sociology, Christian. I. Title.

BT738.R84 2003
177'7--dc21   2002033705

Printed in Canada

To
the members of the Focolare Movement,
and especially to its foundress,
Chiara Lubich,
for the wonderful example they have set
in their practice of loving kindness

Contents

Preface

Traditionally, religion extolled selfless love as the fundamental path to holiness and happiness, secular scholars associated such love with emotional health, and society regarded men and women who practiced it as exemplary role models. However, with the rise of mass culture over the last half-century, the emphasis shifted from self*less* love to the kind of love traditional wisdom had always warned against—self-love.

The new "popular" psychology argued that self-love, far from being dangerous, is the foundation of a healthy, productive life. More extreme adherents of this view claimed that self-esteem and unconditional self-acceptance are the keys to achievement, self-sacrifice is an emotional *illness* ("the disease to please"), and "looking out for number one" is preferable to "looking out for the other guy."

It would be difficult to overstate the impact of this psychology in recent decades. Many educators shifted their focus from increasing knowledge and developing mental skills to helping students feel better about themselves. Numerous publishers substituted guides to self-congratulation for traditional self-improvement books. More than a few ethicists discarded traditional moral standards, including the Ten Commandments and the Golden Rule, and embraced the relativistic belief that wanting to do something makes it acceptable to do. Many mental health professionals declared that nothing is shameful except feelings of shame. Some spiritual counselors modified the tenets of their religions to accommodate the gospel of selfism.

So powerful and pervasive was the self-love message that by the start of the new millennium, self*less* love was widely regarded as hopelessly antiquated, if not downright unwholesome. Only in traditionalist pulpits and publications was it still recommended without reservation.

Then came September 11, 2001 and the holocaust at New York's World Trade Center that shocked the world. Here was barbarism assaulting civilization, a band of zealots driven by blind hatred slaughtering thousands of innocent people. And the subsequent discovery of the plans for biochemical assault would reveal the terrorists' intentions to be even more diabolical than was at first realized.

Yet in the midst of that terrible event, something wonderful occurred. Ordinary people behaved extraordinarily, putting neighbor first, treating others as they would wish to be treated, displaying selfless love. Thousands of people evacuated the Twin Towers in an orderly manner, without trampling others. Many paused in the stairwells to assist less able individuals, in some cases *carrying* them down dozens of flights of stairs. Many who could not flee used their final moments to e-mail or call family members and express their love. Firefighters and police officers ignored their own safety and rushed into the collapsing buildings in the hope of rescuing others.

Scores never returned. A Franciscan priest sacrificed his life administering the last rites to a dying fireman.

Innumerable people rushed to the scene to volunteer, often at great personal cost. Emergency workers pressed themselves beyond exhaustion, corrupting their lungs and tearing flesh from their fingers in an effort to find survivors in the rubble. A Florida man filled his truck with relief items and drove to New York City. After work each day, a business executive spent her nights organizing and facilitating the relief effort. Every morning at 4 or 5 o'clock, thousands of others assembled along surrounding streets just to hold up "Thank you" signs when firefighters, police officers, and volunteers passed by.

In the days and weeks that followed, such demonstrations of loving kindness multiplied. People across the United States and around the world wept, prayed, displayed American flags, and sent messages of condolence and support to the victims' families. Thousands of people donated blood. Hundreds of thousands—from the rich and famous to average working people and even the poor—contributed money to the relief funds. Children held bake sales and set up lemonade stands so that they, too, could give. In a few months the contributions totaled in the billions of dollars.

Not everyone behaved so admirably, of course. A small number of business people took advantage of the situation and raised prices for their goods and services. A tiny minority protested the display of flags, the singing of *God Bless America*, and public prayer for the victims' families. In a few instances, angry individuals harassed Arab-Americans and scrawled anti-Muslim graffiti on mosque walls. And a television host, well known for his irreverence toward religion and traditional values, declared that the terrorists who crashed the planes into the World Trade Center and the Pentagon were more courageous than America's government officials. But the vast majority of people denounced these reactions. Christians and Jews expressed support of their Arab-American neighbors. Non-Muslims helped to clean graffiti from the mosque walls.

Overall, the outpouring of loving kindness in the weeks and months following September 11 affirmed that the human heart's attraction to self*less* love had survived the decades of narcissistic conditioning. Long-clouded truths suddenly became luminous: that self-sacrifice is more satisfying than self-adulation; and that morality, far from being a haven for the repressed or fearful, is in fact a manual for heroism. In an instant, people who had grown up believing that there is no such thing as evil, only different perceptions of what is good, realized that evil truly exists and that we are all challenged to root it from our hearts.

However, the events of September 11 also raised a host of profound questions. Why does it seem to take a tragedy to produce such an outpouring of loving kindness? How can that kindness be cultivated in more normal circumstances? What can be done to prevent self-absorption from blinding us to others' needs? How can our desire to love be translated into concrete action and directed, not just to those we admire or pity, but to all people? These questions are the focus of this book.

Chapter 1

The Universal Ideal

The ancient Greeks were able to speak of love with much greater precision than we can today. They had four words to choose from. *Eros*, the source of our word "erotic," denoted physical passion. *Storge* referred to the love that exists between parent and child or among siblings. *Philia* signified affection between friends. *Agape* denoted respect, empathy and charity toward other people, including strangers and people of races, creeds, and cultures different from one's own. In contrast, we have but a single word to describe our sentiments for ourselves, God, our parents, spouses, children, friends, holiday celebrations, pets, and even our preferences in sports and ice cream.

Unfortunately, the fourth meaning of "love"—respect, empathy, and charity—is the least common one in contemporary usage.[1] To avoid misunderstanding, therefore, anyone who writes about such love is required to include frequent reminders of his or her meaning. One alternative is to use the word *agape* instead, but few writers of English prose, and even fewer readers, are entirely comfortable with that term.

---

1. A glance at a dictionary will confirm this. Most of the definitions of love refer to sensual love, a few to friendship, virtually none to *agape*.

Fortunately, there is a very old English term that encompasses the composite meaning of *agape*. That term is "loving kindness." In addition to suggesting a benevolent *feeling* for humanity in general, "loving kindness" denotes a generous way of *behaving* toward individual people, so it is more concrete and practical than "love." The Hebrew Bible ("Old Testament") contains thirty separate references to the loving kindness of God.[2] "Loving kindness toward all creation" is also a central concept of Buddhism.[3]

Christian scriptures refer to "love" rather than "loving kindness," but the meaning is similar. For example, Jesus commanded his disciples to "love one another as I have loved you" and to "love your enemies, do good to those who hate you, bless those who curse you, pray for those who mistreat you."

Virtually every other religion also has loving kindness as a central theme, though in many cases the term itself is not specifically mentioned. In those cases, some form of the Golden Rule ("Do unto others as you would have them do unto you") is commonly used. The Golden Rule, it should be noted, rests on the understanding that loving kindness to ourselves comes naturally, whereas loving kindness toward others is more difficult, and putting others *before* ourselves requires continuing effort.[4]

---

2. The majority appear in the Book of Psalms.
3. In Pali, the language of the earliest Buddhist texts, the word for loving kindness is *metta*. Contemporary Buddhists still use this word.
4. The idea that self-love must be acquired and continually reinforced is peculiar to *modern western* culture and runs counter to the traditional belief of all cultures, including traditional western culture.

Following are examples of various expressions of this universal ideal, beginning with two from my own faith.

Christianity

"You shall love the Lord your God with all your heart, and with all your soul, and with all your mind." This is the great and foremost commandment. The second is like it, "You shall love your neighbor as yourself."

Matthew, 22:37-9

God is love and he who abides in love abides in God, and God in him. . . . If someone says "I love God," and hates his brother, he is a liar; for the one who does not love his brother whom he has seen, cannot love God whom he has not seen.

1 John, 4:16, 20

Baha'i

And if your eyes are turned towards justice, choose for your neighbor that which you would choose for yourself.

Epistle to the Son of the Wolf, 30

Buddhism

Hurt not others in ways that you would find hurtful.

Tripitaka Udana-varga, 5:18

Confucianism

Tse-kung asked, "Is there one word that can serve as a principle of conduct for life?" Confucius replied, "It is the word '*shu*' — reciprocity. Do not impose on others what you yourself do not desire."

Analects, 15.23

Hinduism

One should not behave towards others in a way which is disagreeable to oneself. This is the essence of morality. All other activities are due to selfish desire.

Mahabharata, Anusasana Parva, 113.8

Islam

Not one of you is a believer until he desires for his brother what he desires for himself.

40 Hadith of an-Nawawi, 13

Jainism

One should treat all beings as he himself would be treated.

Agamas Sutrakritanga 1.10.13

Judaism

What is hateful to you, do not do to your neighbor: that is the whole Torah; all the rest of it is commentary; go and learn.

Rabbi Hillel, Talmud, Shabbat, 31a

Native American

Do not wrong or hate your neighbor.

Pima Proverb

Shintoism

Be charitable to all beings, love is the representative of God.

Ko-ji-ki Hachiman Kasuga

Sikhism

We obtain salvation by loving our fellow man and God.

Granth Japji, 21

Taoism

That nature only is good when it shall not do unto another whatever is not good for its own self.

Avesta: Dadistan-i-dink, 94:5

Unitarian-Universalism

I believe that what unites us as Unitarian Universalists is our spirit of love for neighbor, and a recognition that everyone is our neighbor.

Jan K. Nielsen

Zoroastrianism

Whatever is disagreeable to yourself do not do unto others.

Shayast-na-Shayast, 13:29

Secular Affirmation

Religious exhortations to love one's neighbor may impress religious readers, but other readers understandably prefer secular testimony, of which an abundance also exists. Ancient philosophers not only counseled love of neighbor but did so in language remarkably similar to that of religious texts. Here is a brief sampling of these ancient views:

Do not to your neighbor what you would take ill from him.

Pittacus

Avoid doing what you would blame others for doing.

Thales

What you wish your neighbors to be to you, such be also to them.

Sextus

Do not do to others that which would anger you if others did it to you.

Socrates

We should conduct ourselves toward others as we would have them act toward us.

Aristotle

Cherish reciprocal benevolence, which will make you as anxious for another's welfare as your own.

Aristippus of Cyrene

Treat your inferiors as you would be treated by your superiors.

Seneca

The law imprinted on the hearts of all men is to love the members of society as themselves.

Unknown Roman Author

Many modern psychologists concur with the ancients, including Rollo May, Erich Fromm, Abraham Maslow, and William Glasser.[5] Maslow regarded giving and receiving love as a fundamental human need. Glasser's

---

5. There have, of course, been dissenters, notably Freud and Skinner. Freud refused to acknowledge any kind of love but sexual. Skinner rejected the idea that human beings have the capacity to freely choose their behavior, loving or otherwise. He also rejected the idea that humans possess any special, inherent dignity.

"Reality Therapy" is based on "the need to love and the need to feel we are worthwhile to ourselves and to others." His approach does not dwell on the patient's past but rather on his or her conduct in the present.

Even greater support for love of neighbor is found in the writings of Viennese psychiatrist Viktor Frankl. A survivor of four Nazi concentration camps, Frankl observed human behavior in conditions of utter deprivation. From his own suffering and that of his fellow inmates he learned that emotional health depends not on the conditions of our lives but on our attitude toward them. He wrote, "We [inmates] had to learn . . . that it did not really matter what we expected from life, but rather what life expected from us. . . . Life ultimately means taking the responsibility to find the right answer to its problems and to fulfill the tasks which it constantly sets for each individual."

The concentration camp experience persuaded Frankl that one human drive is deeper and more basic than all others, including the sex drive and the drive for power. That is the drive to discover *meaning* in our lives. This discovery occurs when we forget ourselves and embrace "a cause to serve or another person to love." The significance of love became especially clear to Frankl one day while he trudged to a slave labor site, ill-clad and freezing, with his fellow inmates. Suddenly, he experienced a vivid mental image of his wife and, despite his suffering, "grasped the meaning of the greatest secret that human poetry and belief have to impart: *The salvation of man is through love and in love.*"

Why Loving Kindness Isn't Lived

The fact that loving kindness is a universal theme in religion, philosophy, and psychology raises vexing questions: Why is history filled with hateful deeds? Why have the various Christian denominations regarded one another with suspicion and, in many cases, hostility? Why do so many Jews and Arab Muslims still despise each other? (What makes this question particularly perplexing is that both Jews and Arabs claim descendance from a common patriarch, Abraham.) Why are many Christians, Jews, and Muslims dismissive and even contemptuous of Buddhists and Hindus? Why are non-loving tendencies such as prejudice, discrimination, and incivility so resistant to reform in virtually every culture?

The answer is that we human beings are an imperfect species, prone by our very nature to confusion, error, and evil. In some traditions, particularly Jewish and Christian, this imperfection is regarded as a permanent flaw resulting from the "original sin" of our first parents against God. Scholars may disagree in their interpretations of the specific character and import of that offense, and skeptics may dismiss the biblical account of it as myth. Nevertheless, the reality of human imperfection cannot reasonably be denied. The evidence for it is both too abundant and too easily confirmed:

• Human *knowledge* is imperfect. History has proved that the more deeply any field of study is probed, the more we appreciate how much remains unknown.

• Human *creativity* is imperfect. Every concept, process, or product ever invented is open to improvement. The vast majority of patents are issued for modifications of existing things rather than for entirely new inventions and, no matter how old the invention, such modifications show no sign of abating. Think, for example, of the still continuing evolution of writing instruments from the stylus, or lighting devices from the torch.

• Human *perception* is imperfect. What we learn from parents and teachers often creates preconceptions that distort what we see, hear, and experience thereafter. Even when we manage to control this distortion, distractions and lapses in attention can leave gaps in perception that capricious imagination rushes to fill.

• Human *memory* is imperfect. We tend to forget unpleasant experiences or to refashion them to our liking. Thus we remember what we *wish* we had said or *ought to* have done rather than what we actually said or did. Because this reconstruction of our experiences is often unconscious, the confidence we place in our recollections is largely unwarranted.

• Human *judgment* is imperfect. Although we are capable of forming opinions responsibly, on the basis of careful analysis and logical reasoning, we often follow our impulses and urges instead. When that happens, we tend to choose flattering falsehoods over harsh truths.

• Human *will* is imperfect. However much we may want and strive for any ideal, we often find it difficult to reach. Base inclinations incessantly and insidiously undermine our noble intentions, so that even genuine and heartfelt resolutions get broken, sometimes soon after they are made. For example, we begin our day determined not to participate in office gossip, then succumb to the temptation during our first visit to the water cooler. Or we promise ourselves we will be more tolerant of annoyances and frustrations, then gnash our teeth and complain the moment something goes wrong.

Given our imperfect human nature, the relative dearth of loving kindness is hardly surprising, even among those who aspire to this ideal. No doubt there are people who consciously choose to treat others badly. But there are also people who want to behave lovingly but aren't quite sure how to do so, and many others, perhaps a majority, who are already doing so but not as proficiently or consistently as they would like, particularly with "difficult" people.

Let's be realistic—some people seem to work at being unlovable. Cynics and pessimists, for example, who find fault with everything. Name a restaurant and they'll tell you what is wrong with the food. Mention a movie or television show and they'll offer half a dozen reasons why it is not worth seeing. To such people the weather is always uncomfortable, government officials are all corrupt, and the country is on the fast track to ruin. An accomplished cynic can find something to criticize in the most unlikely situations or people. One writer, for instance, argued that Mother Teresa of Calcutta's life of service to the poor and suffering was selfish rather than noble because her motive was to become holy.

Certain other people are even harder to love because their behavior causes not just annoyance or frustration but physical, emotional, or financial injury. For example, backbiters, gossips, and rumormongers. Propagandists, inciters, and other manipulators of people's minds and emotions. Dishonest business people, hustlers, and scam artists. Drunken drivers, harassers, sex offenders, and terrorists.

Such people can make us wish the command to love our neighbor were conditional. For example, we may wish that

Christ had said, "Love your neighbor as yourself *as long as you approve the way they treat you.*" Or that Buddhist scripture read, "Hurt not others in ways that you would find hurtful *unless they hurt you first.*" Or that the unknown Roman author had written, "The law imprinted on the hearts of all men is to love the members of society as themselves, *provided the members of society measure up to their expectations.*"

Wishing aside, however, that is not what was written. Not one of the exhortations to love others noted earlier—religious or secular, ancient or modern—contains an exclusionary clause. All challenge us to love everyone without exception, including those whom we regard as unlovable.[6]

Some Basic Approaches

The next four chapters will present numerous accounts of loving kindness in thoughts, words, actions, and benevolent silences. But before turning to those stories, it may be helpful to examine some basic approaches that can improve the practice of loving kindness.

Recognize Opportunities to Love

Have you ever had an opportunity to risk your life to save another person—for example, to rescue an unconscious woman from a burning car or to swim out into the ocean to save a drowning man? Odds are you haven't, because such dramatic opportunities for loving kindness

---

6. On the other hand, nowhere is it recorded, in writings sacred or profane, that you have to *like* difficult people or enjoy their company.

are rare. Yet dozens of more modest opportunities arise every day. For example, the opportunity to hold a door for someone, volunteering for an onerous task, driving "friendly," sending a note of condolence, expressing gratitude for a kindness, showing patience with a difficult person, and speaking charitably of someone you dislike.

There is a word in Hebrew for such small acts: *mitzvahs.*[7] One who performs many *mitzvahs* is considered a *mensch* or "angel of kindness." To become a *mensch* we need only to take advantage of ordinary, everyday opportunities. If the big opportunity ever arrives, we'll be better prepared for it. And if it *never* does, we'll still have thousands of *mitzvahs* to our credit. No doubt William Penn had something similar in mind when he wrote: "I expect to pass through life but once. If, therefore, there be any kindness I can show, or any good thing I can do to any fellow being, let me do it now, as I shall not pass this way again."

Be More Aware of Other People

Before we can love others, we must acknowledge them as human beings with thoughts and feelings, hopes and aspirations little different from our own. This is not as easy as it may seem. One reason is that popular psychology encourages preoccupation with self—monitoring one's self-esteem, keeping in touch with one's feelings, and "looking out for number one." Other reasons are

---

7. The reference here is to the popular meaning of *mitzvah*. Originally, the term meant "commandment" and included obligations of the law as well as good deeds. (Though the anglicized plural *mitzvahs* is used here, the Hebrew plural is *mitzvot*.)

the fast pace of modern living and the distractions created by modern technology. We may be too busy rushing between activities or too involved with our cell phone and Palm Pilot to pay much attention to the people around us. If we notice them at all, we may regard them as we do ATM machines or parking meters—as convenient or inconvenient *objects*. This habit accounts for much of the rudeness and incivility in modern life.

You may not be able to do much about your busy schedule, but you can become more aware of the people you encounter every day. Remind yourself frequently that they, like you, face difficult challenges and choices, carry emotional burdens, struggle with annoyances and frustrations, experience disappointment and grief. Regard them as fellow seekers of meaning and fulfillment, compatriots in life, and let this perspective show. Acknowledge everyone you meet with a smile and a friendly nod.[8] And when you have occasion to speak to them, be pleasant and courteous. Behave this way not just with people you can profit from cultivating, such as clients and business executives, but also with people who have little or no authority or influence, such as parking lot attendants, sales clerks, and waitresses. One of the best measures of character is how well we treat those who have no power over us.

Expect Less of Others

According to an ancient proverb, "All unhappiness is the result of excessive expectations." This certainly

---

8. In some cases, of course, common sense counsels otherwise. A woman might decide that smiling at a stranger would send an unintended message.

applies to the expectations we have concerning other people. The more we expect of them, the greater the chance that they will disappoint us and that we will become displeased and angry. Those feelings often lead to cruel thoughts, words, and actions, which make us unhappy and, in many cases, ashamed.

Fortunately, to end this cycle of misery we need only lower our expectations of others. Note that the word is *lower* and not *eliminate*. Expecting less doesn't mean abolishing performance standards for our subordinates at work or inviting others (for example, our children) to neglect their responsibilities. It means anticipating other people's oversights and blunders and making appropriate allowance for them. Here is how to do this:

Each day, on rising, remind yourself that one or more things are bound to go wrong at work, at home, or both because people are imperfect and therefore prone to mistakes. Recall, too, how you typically react to *your own* mistakes and oversights. Do you fly into a rage, call yourself stupid or lazy, question your motives, and dredge up past errors to humiliate yourself further? Or do you simply think, "That was foolish. I'm going to try hard to avoid that mistake from now on"? *Surely the latter.*

As you go through each day, be prepared for the people around you to make mistakes and, when they do, treat them exactly as you treat yourself, graciously. When the mistakes are serious or recurrent enough to warrant spoken or written criticism, by all means give it. But be as gentle and constructive as you would be with yourself in the same circumstances.

Apply this approach faithfully and you will become not only more loving to others but also more at peace with yourself.

Control Negative Emotions

No doubt you've heard that it is unhealthy to suppress negative emotions. According to this theory, whenever we feel upset with someone or something, we should express our annoyance, anger, or resentment. Doing so is supposed to purge the negative emotions and make us feel better about the situation and ourselves. This theory is mistaken. Research has shown that expressing negative emotions has the opposite effect. When our negative emotions intensify, we feel *more* hostile toward the people involved, and we become more likely to experience negative emotions in the future.

Everyday experience confirms these research findings. Have you ever had someone cut sharply in front of you on the highway, causing you to slam on your brakes? If you have, and if you expressed your negative feelings aloud, either to yourself or to your passengers, you know how easy it is to *keep on* talking about the matter. One angry word has a way of leading to many more. If you don't force yourself to stop or happen to have your attention diverted, you may still be grumbling about the incident an hour down the road. In fact, you may be angrier at that point than you were initially. Loving thoughts are not likely to intrude on such a mood.

One good reason to control negative emotions, then, is that they create unpleasantness for yourself and others. Another is that they tend to make matters worse instead of better. Think of the statements you most regret having made and the actions you most regret having taken. Chances are, each was caused by an emotional overreaction to a situation, and if you had waited a few hours or days before speaking or acting, you would have been spared your present sorrow and regret. Time tends to put matters into clearer perspective; today's intolerable situation may seem inconsequential tomorrow.

Though the passing of time will generally temper our emotions, it will not automatically bring reason to bear. For that we will need to ask these questions: Is the situation really worth being upset about? Who is responsible for it and to what extent? What is the best explanation of what happened? What choices do I have in responding? Which response best meets the ideal of loving kindness to all involved?

Keep in mind that, though we cannot control what life brings to us, we can choose how we respond to it. The Dalai Lama tells of a Tibetan scholar who, following the Chinese occupation of his country, "spent more than twenty years in prison enduring the most terrible treatment including torture." Through those years the scholar managed to smuggle letters out of prison to his students. The students said the letters "contained the most profound teachings on love and compassion they had ever encountered." The scholar had chosen to respond positively to a terrible situation.

Be Quick to Forgive

The prayer that Jesus taught his disciples, the *Our Father,* includes the words "forgive us our trespasses as we forgive those who trespass against us."[9] Most of us should shudder when making this petition, for we are more inclined to condemn than to forgive offenders. And once we act on that inclination and retaliate, forgiveness

---

9. Other translations say "forgive us our debts as we forgive our debtors"; still others, "forgive us our wrongs as we forgive those who have wronged us."

becomes even more difficult because we then blame the offender for "causing" us to act ignobly.

Robert Fulghum relates a case that dramatically illustrates this difficulty. In 1937, Gertrude Jamison's dog jumped over a hedge and nipped newsboy A. D. Thompson on the heel. He called the Humane Society and reported the attack. Offended that he did so, Jamison decided to make his life miserable by placing as many as fifteen nuisance phone calls to him every day. Even after she was jailed for harassment and had a court-ordered padlock put on her phone, she found other ways to pester him. This went on for years. In fact, she was still at it *forty-five years later,* at age eighty-four. She had, quite literally, surrendered her life to a single negative emotion.

Now imagine a different scenario. Suppose that after becoming angry over Thompson's call to the Humane Society, Jamison had reflected on the entire incident and reasoned, "Though I don't think he should have reported my dog, he probably thought he was doing the right thing. So even though I feel offended, I forgive him."[10] This simple reaction would have spared Thompson mental anguish and Jamison herself forty-five years of self-punishing, soul-shriveling resentment.

Forgiving others is appropriate even when the offense is heinous and the offender is not remorseful. Not long ago I heard the story of a Congolese man who, on learning that his daughter had been raped, murdered, and thrown into the river by marauding outlaws, immediately called his other children together and prayed for God *to forgive the perpetrators.* At about the same time, in an American

---

10. Of course, it could be argued that Thompson committed a public service rather than an offense and that Jamison owed *him* an apology for her dog's attack.

courtroom, the parents of a murder victim appeared at the sentencing of her murderer and begged for leniency, explaining that their daughter would have wanted them to do so.

These stories recall the older, even more dramatic case of Maria Goretti. In 1902, at age eleven, Maria was stabbed fourteen times by a twenty-year-old neighbor, Alessandro Serenelli, for refusing his sexual advances. The next day, just before she died, Maria forgave him. Thirty years later, after Alessandro had served his prison sentence, he visited Maria's mother and begged her forgiveness. She explained that she had already forgiven him many years earlier and proceeded to welcome him into her home and treat him as a son.

"In every pardon there is love," as the Welsh proverb rightly notes. There is also improved mental and even physical health for the one who forgives. Financier and elder statesman Bernard Baruch understood this. When he was well into his nineties, he shared his prescription for longevity: "One of the secrets of a long and fruitful life is to forgive everybody everything every night before you go to bed."

Chapter 2

Loving Kindness in Thoughts

The game-worn, autographed John Elway football jersey hung in a glass-enclosed frame on Casey's condominium wall. It was one of his most valuable and cherished sports memorabilia. When Tommy, the thirteen-year-old son of a friend, first saw it, he couldn't take his eyes off it because the Denver Broncos were his favorite team and John Elway was his hero. Then two years later, Tommy sustained a serious head injury in a high school football game and lay in a coma from which doctors were uncertain he would ever emerge.

From that moment on, every time Casey looked at the Elway jersey, he thought of Tommy and how excited he had been about it. "Perhaps I should give him the jersey," Casey thought. At first he resisted; after all, it was worth almost three thousand dollars and had great sentimental value. Yet the thought grew more insistent: "How happy Tommy would be to own that jersey. What hope and encouragement it would give him in the long process of rehabilitation." Finally Casey resolved that when Tommy came out of the coma, he would give him the jersey. And a few weeks later he made good on his resolution, with a note that said "John Elway was statistically considered the greatest comeback player in NFL history. May the shirt off his back and God's blessing motivate you to make the greatest comeback of your life."

Not only did the gift have the expected effect with Tommy; it also brought unexpected joy to Casey. He later commented that the gratification he experienced from giving away the jersey far outweighed its monetary and sentimental value, for giving it made him "feel God's pleasure."

Thought Patterns Differ

Casey's experience illustrates an important fact. Words and deeds do not spring from the void; they originate in the mind, consciously or subconsciously, and represent some mixture of imagination, emotion, and reason. Unfortunately, not all mental processing results in loving thoughts.

The story is told of a man who found himself on a lonely country road at 2 a.m., with a flat tire and no jack. Remembering that he had passed a farmhouse a mile before, he began walking back to it. "I hope the farmer has a jack to loan me," he said to himself. When he had gone a half-mile, another thought arose: "He'll probably be upset being awakened at this hour." His imagination chewed on that for the next half-mile, and he soon manufactured a scenario in which the farmer cursed him for waking him and threatened to call the police. "It's pretty sad that a person in need should be treated so ungraciously," the man muttered to himself as he knocked on the farmhouse door. Then the door opened, but before the farmer had a chance to speak, the man shouted, "You can keep your lousy jack" and stormed away.

Most of us can identify with that man, even if we've never behaved quite so foolishly. We tend to conduct our mental affairs casually, if not downright sloppily. Thus we often fall into patterns of thought that are less than fair and therefore less than loving, such as assuming the worst about others, judging them hastily, and reading into their behavior intentions and motivations that may not be there.

Suppose, for example, that you have a friend with many good qualities but one that bothers you a great deal—his frugality. Though he is always ready to accept others' offers to pick up a check or treat him to a concert or ballgame, he seldom reciprocates. "Does he really think he is kidding anyone?" you wonder. "Maybe he enjoys taking advantage of other people's goodness. Money is probably more important to him than friendship." And so on. The less kind your thoughts, the madder they make you; the madder they make you, the less loving you feel; and the less loving you feel, the less likely will you be to think, speak, and act kindly about your friend.

Challenging Unkind Thoughts

It may seem that your friend's behavior leaves you no choice but to think ill of him, but that is not so. Circumstances may *suggest* a conclusion, but they don't *dictate* it. You always remain free to pursue other lines of thought and embrace other opinions. You could consider the possibility that your friend's frugality is unintentional. Perhaps he learned it in childhood and he is unaware that others, including you, find it offensive. Perhaps he demonstrates his gratitude in other ways than monetary, such as in giving his time and talent to his friends and benefactors. The moment you decide that one or both of these explanations are plausible, his frugality will become more tolerable.

Let's consider some other situations. Imagine that you are at a business meeting and have just presented your position on the issue under discussion when a colleague explains, point by point, why she disagrees with you. Your first response is to think, "Thanks a lot. Some friend you are, making me look bad in front of the boss." At this point you might ask yourself, "What was she supposed to do, stifle her own idea, even though she felt confident it was a better response to the issue?" The obvious answer is no—refusing to share her idea would be a disservice to the company. This realization would help you form a more charitable view of her.

Next, suppose you are at a party with your spouse and he's telling a story you've heard him tell a dozen times before. You think, "I can't believe he's telling that story again. I'm sure everybody's heard it, some more than once. I'm so embarrassed." You might challenge this reaction as follows: "He surely is not repeating himself on purpose. More likely, he just forgets whom he has told what. That's no big deal, I forget a lot of things myself. Besides, he gets such pleasure making people laugh." This thought would very likely dissolve your feeling of annoyance.

Now imagine yourself receiving a telephone solicitation at the usual time, just as you are sitting down to eat dinner. Your first impulse is to say something sarcastic, like "Thank you for interrupting my dinner," or to berate the caller, or simply to slam the receiver down. Before acting on this impulse you might say to yourself, "What a difficult way to earn a living, having to repeat the same spiel over and over, literally thousands of times, and then being cursed at and insulted." That thought might prompt you to find a gentler, friendlier way to say you aren't interested.

Are there any extreme situations in which the initial negative thought is so appropriate that there is no point in challenging it? The terrorist attack on New York City's World Trade Center would certainly seem to be such a situation. The immediate response of many people—to hate what was done *and* the people who did it—may have seemed to be the only sensible reaction. But further reflection, particularly on the fact that the perpetrators had been brainwashed to believe they were serving God, suggests a different reaction—hating what was done yet *pitying* the misguided individuals who were duped into doing it.

Some people reject such a reaction, fearing that compassion for evildoers is equivalent to condoning evil. Certainly, cases could be cited that fit this formula. The most obvious example is misguided judges who give light sentences for heinous crimes and thereby both encourage criminals and insult their victims. Even in such cases, however, the error lies not in pitying the perpetrator but in trivializing the offense. Compassion and justice are not mutually exclusive.

Cultivating Loving Thoughts

It is much easier to love humanity in the abstract than to love individual human beings, because humanity in the abstract is never annoying or offensive, whereas individual human beings are often both. Time and again they dispute your ideas, challenge your pleasant self-deceptions, frustrate your plans and intentions, wound your ego, and in some cases cause more serious harm. There are, however, strategies you can use to cultivate loving thoughts despite these obstacles. The following ones are especially effective.

Resist Negative Influences

Unless you are a recluse, you are bombarded by information all day, every day, and much of it celebrates unkind thoughts and deeds. "Action" films depict villains doing heinous deeds, heroes retaliating, and the outcome having less to do with decency and nobility than with proficiency in hitting, kicking, shooting, and setting off explosions. Situation comedies are typically little more than extended exchanges of witty (or, just as often, witless) insults. Dramas often portray manipulating others and breaking vows and obligations as normal and therefore justifiable behavior. The lyrics of certain types of music tend to be not only unloving but unmistakably hateful.

As if fictional unkindness were not enough, the news is overflowing with reports of *actual* mayhem. Such stories are given preference over accounts of kindness and decency not so much because there is more evil than good in the world (there probably isn't) as because sensationalism sells.[1]

Exposure to violent entertainment, sensational news, and rude discourse may not have a direct, dramatic effect

---

1. The news media's claim that they are "providing what the public wants" is partly true, but they are also stimulating the public's appetite for what they provide.

on you. But it can certainly familiarize you with patterns of unkindness and invite imitation. In response, you can try to become more aware of these negative influences, look for indications that they may be affecting your thinking, and make a special effort to resist them.

Give the Benefit of the Doubt

Some years ago a friend of my wife phoned her on a number of occasions over a period of a few weeks. Whenever I answered, the woman would say, "Is Barbara there?" The first time this happened, I said nothing to my wife but thought privately that since the woman knew me it was rude of her not to address me by name and exchange a pleasantry. When it happened again, I was more bothered. After several times, I shared my annoyance with my wife. "I don't recall ever having done anything to warrant her refusing me the simple courtesy of acknowledging my existence," I complained. Not surprisingly, expressing the thought made me feel even more offended.

Fortunately, my wife said nothing to her friend about my hurt feelings because a few weeks later the woman confided to her that whenever I answered the phone, she felt guilty for disturbing my writing. When my wife told me, I realized that all the while I had been thinking unkind thoughts about the woman, she had been thinking *kind* thoughts about me. If I had given her the benefit of the doubt, I would have spared myself a lot of unpleasant emotion and the eventual embarrassment of being proved both ungenerous and wrong.

The benefit of the doubt is appropriate whenever it is uncertain that an unkind assessment is warranted. An elderly patient in a cancer hospital cursed and screamed at the nurses and bit and scratched them when they took her pulse or blood pressure. At first they tried to hold her down when doing these procedures; eventually, they used restraints. Because of her behavior, the woman became known as "the witch" and the staff felt they had good reason for disliking her. However, one nurse, Darlene, was willing to give her the benefit of the doubt. Whenever she saw the woman, she spoke softly, called her by name, and touched her gently. The woman quickly calmed down. Soon she let Darlene help her into a chair, comb her hair, and put a ribbon in it. When Darlene told the other nurses about this, they reconsidered their assessment and gave the woman another chance. By the time she was well enough to leave the hospital, she had become one of the staff's favorite patients.

The lesson in the elderly woman's case is well summed up in the advice a pastor gave me several decades ago: "Never attribute to malice what can reasonably be attributed to fear, inattention, or ignorance." This wise advice can be applied to many situations. Suppose, for example, someone you've known for years passes you on the street without speaking to you, and you are inclined to think that he purposely snubbed you. Ask yourself whether another explanation is possible; for example, that he was daydreaming or absorbed in some problem, such as a family member's illness or his own financial difficulties. Since you can't be sure, give him the benefit of the doubt.

Similarly, if a department store clerk leaves you standing while she waits on someone who came in after you, regard her behavior as an honest mistake, the kind we all make from time to time, rather than an intentional offense. And if a normally polite co-worker speaks sharply to you, attribute her words to frustration about something else rather than animosity toward you.

On those occasions when circumstances make it impossible to give the benefit of the doubt, use humor to temper your unkind thought. If a speeding car cuts in front of you, say to yourself, "I hope the driver makes it to his safe driving class on time." And the next time a celebrity makes a disparaging remark about religion, think "What a clever demonstration of the fact that money can't buy class."

Consider the Other Person's Perspective

Unkind thoughts can often be traced to narrowness of perspective. The problem occurs quite naturally. Our own experiences and thoughts are vivid to us; other people's are at best shadowy. Only by making a conscientious effort can we see and feel as they do (and even then only imperfectly). But the effort is well worth making because it can provide a basis for loving kindness, as the following story illustrates.

Brad, a teenager, felt overburdened by the chores his mother expected him to complete. Not only did he find a list of them waiting for him each day after school; his mother often called him from work to add others. Resentful, he imagined her sitting at work thinking up tasks for him. In retaliation, he would procrastinate until the last half-hour, and then do his chores quickly and haphazardly. Often as not, he managed to "forget" one or two tasks, which of course led to his mother expressing displeasure.

Then one day it occurred to Brad to look at the situation from his mother's perspective. A single parent, she had to work hard to support them. What she expected of him, he reasoned, was really very little in comparison with what she gave, and she assigned him tasks not to make his life difficult but because she needed his help. Brad decided to regard his chores as opportunities to express his gratitude rather than as a burden. He began to work more diligently and each day tried to do something extra. When his mother noticed the change in him and started complimenting him, a sense of pride and satisfaction replaced his feeling of resentment. Before long, he no longer dreaded his chores but actually looked forward to them.

This approach is helpful in a variety of situations. For example, by seeing your workplace from your employer's perspective, you may appreciate the need for regulations and procedures you previously thought to be arbitrary. By adopting your pastor's perspective on church affairs, you may realize that many of the criticisms parishioners make about his decisions are unfair. And by putting yourself in the place of a family member with whom you don't get along and seeing the dividing issues as she sees them, you may find a basis for thinking more kindly of her and settling your differences.

Reflect On Your Experiences

Devote some time regularly, daily if possible, to pondering your experiences with loving kindness. Include not only experiences in which you gave it, but also those in which you received it and those you have read about. The story of how Scott Adams became a successful cartoonist is a good example of the latter.

As Adams tells it, when he was just an aspiring cartoonist and unsure how to get his work published, he wrote to a successful cartoonist, Jack Cassady, enclosing a sample of his work and asking for advice. Cassady wrote back answering the questions and offering some suggestions. Adams was grateful and followed the advice but, as often happens with artists and writers, his cartoons were rejected. Disappointed, Adams decided to give up cartooning. About a year later, however, he received an unexpected follow-up letter from Cassady encouraging him once again to submit his work for publication. That act of loving kindness was enough to motivate Adams to start cartooning again. This time the ending was different. The strips he created became the popular Dilbert cartoon.

Reflecting on such acts of loving kindness and the good they bring about can give you ideas for similar acts and encourage you to carry them out.

Set Specific Goals

The clearer our goals are, the better our chance of making them the focus of our thoughts. This is as true with the practice of loving kindness as it is with any other worthwhile challenge. One way of making our goals clear is to write them out in our own words. Another is to find a poem or prayer that expresses them. Following are three prayers that millions of people have found helpful. Although they represent very different religious traditions—Buddhist, Baha'i, and Christian—they are remarkably similar in focus.

Prayer of the Dalai Lama

> May I become at all times, both now and forever
> A protector for those without protection
> A guide for those who have lost their way
> A ship for those with oceans to cross
> A sanctuary for those in danger
> A lamp for those without light
> A place of refuge for those who lack shelter
> And a servant to all in need.

Baha'i Prayer

> Be generous in prosperity,
> and thankful in adversity.
> Be fair in judgment,
> and guarded in thy speech,
> Be a lamp unto those who walk in darkness,
> and a home to the stranger.
> Be eyes to the blind, and a guiding light
> unto the feet of the erring
> Be a breath of life to the body of humankind,
> a dew to the soil of the human heart,
> and a fruit upon the tree of humility.

Prayer of Saint Francis

> Lord, make me an instrument of your peace.
> Where there is hatred, let me sow love;
> Where there is injury, pardon;
> Where there is doubt, faith;
> Where there is despair, hope;
> Where there is darkness, light;
> Where there is sadness, joy;
>
> O Divine Master,
> grant that I may not so much seek
> To be consoled as to console,
> To be understood as to understand,
> To be loved as to love.
> For it is in giving that we receive,
> It is in pardoning that we are pardoned,
> And it is in dying that we are born to eternal life.

Reading your personal goal statement or reciting one of these prayers every day will keep the goal of loving kindness clearly in mind and help you achieve it.

Anticipate Setbacks

No matter how diligent our efforts to cultivate loving kindness in our thoughts, unkind and even hateful thoughts are bound to recur, often when we least expect them. Remember the case of the frugal friend presented earlier in the chapter. We saw how by challenging unkind thoughts you could dispel them and accept your friend's frugality as, at worst, a minor fault. Let's assume that approach was successful for you. Ever since, whenever he has displayed his frugality, you have been able to smile inwardly and overlook it. But he just did it again, and though the circumstances were no different now than they were a dozen times before, your old anger has returned and you must subdue it all over again.

Something similar can occur with an old grievance. Though you may have long since forgiven the offender, merely recalling the offense months or years later can awaken your resentment. When that happens you may doubt the sincerity of your forgiveness, but the more likely explanation is that your decision to forgive, having come later, is contained in a separate memory. The solution is to remind yourself that you have already forgiven the person and have no intention of reversing that decision.

Never allow your setbacks to discourage you or undermine your resolve to cultivate loving thoughts. The human mind is like a garden that needs constant tending to prevent weeds from choking out the flowers.

Chapter 3

Loving Kindness in Words

My first job after college was as a social case worker in Albany, New York. One of my assigned cases was an elderly couple who lived on the top floor of a shabby tenement building. On my first visit, the husband was visibly sad and the reason was obvious. He was concerned for his thin, frail wife, who sat in a rocking chair, rocking and sobbing. After a few awkward minutes, the old man motioned me out into the hall.

"Please understand that my wife is suffering from cancer," he explained, "but something far more painful is troubling her. Today is her birthday and she realizes that no one will call or send a greeting."

He went on to explain that he had once owned a large hotel in an Adirondack Mountain resort town. Business had been good and he and his wife prospered. They had one child, a son, to whom they gave everything money could buy, including fine cars and an excellent education. Now they were on welfare and the son, a successful lawyer who also owned a large hardware store, not only would have nothing to do with them but also kept his grandchildren from them.

"Do you have children, young man?" the old man asked. I shook my head no. "If you ever should," he exhorted, "please profit from my unfortunate experience and don't be too indulgent. You will spoil them and regret it for the rest of your life."

That incident occurred over forty-five years ago, and yet I remember every detail of it as if it happened yesterday, for it was a profound experience. The old man was willing to share the most painful lesson of his life with a stranger in the hope that he could profit from it. His warning, which I have tried my best to heed, was a memorable example of loving kindness in words.

Another memorable experience occurred when a new caseworker joined the agency, a man who had coincidentally taught me Freshman English in college four years earlier. I had been impressed then with his mastery of the English language and his classroom manner. Unfortunately, it developed that, despite his considerable talent, he was more interested in dissolute living than in pursuing a graduate degree. When he was arrested in a gambling raid, he lost his teaching job.

Now, as a caseworker, he seemed more quiet and subdued. Though not unfriendly, he kept to himself, rarely said more than was necessary, and never discussed personal matters. Then one day, to my surprise, he took me aside and said, "Whatever you do, don't waste your talent as I did. Go to graduate school." He didn't elaborate and he never repeated the message. He didn't have to. I appreciated at once how difficult it was for him to mention his mistakes, especially to a former student, and that doing so was an act of loving kindness. Soon afterward, I followed his advice and enrolled in graduate school.

The Power of Words

No doubt you have had similar experiences, in which ordinary words spoken in ordinary situations had an extraordinary impact on you. Such experiences demonstrate that a simple phrase spoken in loving kindness can be as powerful in its own way as the more memorable words of an Abraham Lincoln, John F. Kennedy, or Martin Luther King, Jr. Ordinary words have the power to lift sunken spirits, restore hope, and provide the motivation necessary to undertake difficult tasks.

Jennifer, who runs a homeless shelter, was talking to a despondent man. He explained that he had lost his father and brother in auto accidents, then lost his job, and was now separated from his wife and family. "I feel the need to pray," he said, "and I try to every day. But I just can't bring myself to promise that I'll never sin again because I know very well that I will." Jennifer replied, "Maybe you should just pray, 'God, be merciful to me, a sinner.'" Such a modest suggestion seemed so inadequate that she was almost embarrassed to have made it. Yet the man's eyes lit up. And whenever he saw her after that he would always mention that little prayer and tell her how helpful it was.

Piyadhammo, a Buddhist monk in Thailand, tells of the time when he overslept and missed a teaching by his Abbot. He feared what the Abbot might say the next time he met him, but when that time came, the Abbot merely smiled kindly and said, "sleep is delicious." In that gentle observation Piyadhammo found comfort and encouragement.

Brenda, who does outreach work with the elderly, was touched when a client said, "Thank you for dignifying my existence." Edna was delighted when her married daughter announced, "Having children of my own has made me appreciate what a great Mom you have been to me." And Peter, an eight-year-old who was teased by his classmates because he was poor and shabbily dressed, was thrilled when a little girl in his class whispered, "I feel bad when kids say mean things to you, because I think you are a nice person."

For Marie, a volunteer at a soup kitchen, the uplifting words were scribbled on a napkin and pressed into her hand by an elderly man. The people who came for food were often unappreciative. On many days, they complained about the quality of the food, the size of the portions, the length of the lines, the people around them, and so on. Early one Christmas morning, when Marie had taken time away from her family to work at the soup kitchen, the grumbling was especially bad. Depressed, she began to wonder, "Why do I bother?" At that very moment, the old man gave her the napkin and walked away. She opened it and read, "When you care for strangers, you will be visited by angels." These words, which echoed a familiar biblical passage, renewed her sense of purpose.

The Ripple Effect

Just as pebbles tossed in a lake create ripples that extend far beyond the point of impact, small expressions of loving kindness can touch lives far removed in time and place. For example, when Karla was fourteen her family moved and she had to attend a different high school. Since her siblings had all graduated, she had to face this challenge alone. Her apprehension made her resentful and she began to be sullen and uncooperative around her mother.

One day when Karla was particularly unloving, her mother told her a story about a woman who had fallen out of love with her husband and was thinking about leaving him. The woman's pastor had advised her to try an experiment first—to *act as if* she loved her husband—and see what would happen. The woman did as he suggested and, to her surprise, fell in love with her husband once again. At the end of the story, Karla's mother added, "I can sense that you don't love me right now, but if you start acting as if you do, maybe your feelings will change."

Karla took her mother's advice and soon discovered that she really did love her mother. But that is not the end of the story. Many years later, when Karla was almost forty, she sent her mother this e-mail message: "Remember how you told me the story about the woman who fell out of love with her husband, and how you asked me to do as she did? I've always thought there was great wisdom in those words and I want you to know I've shared them with many people over the years. In fact, I just had occasion to share them with my son."

Simple Yet Powerful Expressions

Many people find it difficult to express loving thoughts in words. They may have no difficulty communicating clearly and directly about everyday matters, such as the weather, the price of gasoline, and the state of world affairs. They may also be adept, and even enthusiastic, in voicing objections, complaints, and criticisms. Yet when it comes to kinder, gentler expressions, they experience verbal block. Men seem to have this problem more often than women, but women are by no means immune to it.

The best way to become comfortable expressing loving kindness in words is to start small, employing simple expressions that are sure to be well received by others and relatively easy to say, and then moving on to more difficult expressions. Here are some simple ones.

"Good morning"

If you are a busy person, you may be so absorbed in your thoughts that you ignore the person you see every day at the bus or subway station, the newspaper vendor, the maintenance worker, and even the person in the next office. But it costs nothing to offer a cheerful "good morning" and perhaps to add an upbeat comment about the weather or wish the person a "nice day." Of course, some would protest that such words are empty or trite. But that is true only if you mean them to be so. If you intend them to acknowledge the other person as your fellow human being and neighbor, and if your sentiment is genuine, they will convey loving kindness.

"Thank you"

Have you ever stopped to realize that the person who held a door open for you *freely chose* to do so? Or that the person with the full shopping cart who looked at your three items and said "Please go in front of me" was moved by kindness rather than compulsion? Or that the person who had as much right as you to the parking space but waved for you to take it instead did not *have* to behave so generously? Such acts are freely chosen out of the goodness of the heart. Saying "thank you" to those people lets them know that you don't take their benevolence for granted.

But don't let your thanks giving end with those everyday situations. Thank all the people you encounter every day who serve you cheerfully and well—the grocery clerks, bank tellers, police officers, repairmen, doctors, nurses, and all the others. The fact that these people are paid for their services should not make you any less appreciative of what they do.

Thank, too, the people who have made a special contribution to your knowledge and happiness, notably your teachers and mentors. If you have lost contact with them, make an effort to find them and express your gratitude. Finally, and in some ways most important, thank the people you live or work closely with for their faithfulness and support.

"Congratulations"

The obvious occasions for offering congratulations are marriage, graduation from school or college, winning the lottery, and having a baby. But there are lots of other appropriate occasions, as well, such as earning a good grade in a difficult college course, completing a demanding work assignment ahead of schedule, receiving a promotion, or any other situation involving personal achievement or good fortune.

If you feel awkward saying "congratulations," try writing it in a card or letter. A couple of lines will do nicely. Just say, "Congratulations on your recent promotion. It was well deserved." Or "I was delighted to hear that you won the club tennis tournament. Overcoming the strong competition at this year's tournament was a real accomplishment." If you have trouble composing the message, chances are you can find a commercial greeting card that does it for you.

"What can I do to help?"

These words say that you care enough to lighten the other person's burden. When you ask this, the person may automatically say "Nothing, I'm fine," even if she is not. So be ready with a specific suggestion. If her car is being repaired, offer to give her a ride. If she is laid up with an injury, offer to go shopping for her, prepare a meal, or walk the dog.

"I understand how you feel"

Susan, age twelve, was waiting to see the school nurse when a younger girl came in and sat down beside her. The girl was in tears, so Susan asked her what was wrong. The girl explained that her uncle had just died and she felt very sad. Susan said that she remembered having the same feeling when her grandfather died. While Susan was saying this, the little girl stopped crying and listened intently. Then she thanked Susan, adding that knowing others experienced the same kind of sadness made it a little easier to bear.

Whenever someone you know is experiencing sadness, follow Susan's example and find a way to express your understanding. If you can't express the thought in person, do it in writing, either in your own words or with an appropriate card.

Once you become comfortable with these simple words of loving kindness, you'll be ready for words that are also sure to evoke a favorable response but, for one reason or another, you may find more difficult to express.

"You look good"/"That looks good"

Many people are miserly with compliments. If they notice that a friend's hair or clothes look especially nice, they admire in secret, refusing to share their reaction. If someone returns to work from vacation looking tanned and rested, they may manage to ask "Was the weather good?" or "Did you have a good time?" But they can't bring themselves to say "You look wonderful." If someone has reached the goal of her diet, they'll either pretend they don't see or, worse, comment that her clothes don't fit well anymore.

These people often have the same difficulty saying that someone's *things* are attractive—the furniture or knick-knacks in someone's home, for example, or her painting or sculpture.

If you find it difficult to compliment others, you need to realize that compliments are a way of bringing joy to others without cost to you. The next time you find yourself thinking that someone or something looks good, don't hide the thought; put it into words.

"You're right"

If you watch TV talk-shows, you've probably noticed how seldom the hosts and guests say "you're right" or "I agree." Whether the subject is the federal budget, a controversy among local school board members, or the merits of a movie, the participants act as if loyalty to their position demands total disagreement with the opposing viewpoint. This unfortunate approach to discussion is also encountered in many homes, offices, and meeting places.

It's natural to want to be totally right. However, in most disputes each side is partly right and partly wrong. In such cases, even if you are mostly right, you can admit where you are wrong, and you can make that admission generous rather than grudging.

"I care about you"

When Matt was eighteen, he became convinced that his parents' house rules were oppressive, so he went to live with a friend, without telling his parents where he was going. A few days later, he was shocked to see his father at the friend's door. When Matt opened the door, his father said, "I came to find you because I care about you and want to be sure you are all right." Then he left.

Matt realized at once how difficult it had been for his father to overcome his pride, go searching for him, suppress his feelings of disappointment and annoyance, and express his love. Humbled by his father's example, Matt returned home the next day. Looking back on the incident eight years later, he decided that he had been rude and rebellious, which made him even more grateful for his father's loving kindness.

There are many ways of communicating that you care. For example, one of Teresa's second grade students had a cleft palate. Despite Teresa's best efforts to encourage the other students to be sensitive, some of them teased and mocked the little girl. One day Teresa was conducting an informal hearing test by whispering a sentence into each student's ear and seeing if he or she understood. When she came to that little girl, however, instead of using one of the standard sentences, she whispered, "I wish you were my little girl." Realizing that her teacher cared for her, the little girl beamed.

"I'm sorry"

Someone once termed these words the most painful to express in any language. That may well be correct. Saying them violates a cardinal tendency of human nature—blaming others for everything that goes wrong. This foolish habit goes all the way back to Adam blaming Eve, and Eve, in turn, blaming the serpent. I say foolish because when we refuse to admit that the fault may lie with us rather than with others, we make it impossible to take responsibility for our behavior, overcome our faults and weaknesses, and heal wounded relationships.

The challenge of admitting our offenses is greatest when we are only partly in the wrong. June's story is a good illustration of this. For years, June and her husband and children included her sister-in-law on their family vacations, even though the woman was domineering and had an unusually negative outlook. June had always done her best to tolerate the woman, mostly for the sake of her husband. But after June's husband died, she arranged to spend her time with her children at a favorite vacation spot and share memories without the sister-in-law. Predictably, a friend of her sister-in-law was visiting there at the time and couldn't wait to let her know that she had been left out.

The sister-in-law promptly fired off a note of protest, arguing that the place and the people also held memories for her and she was deeply hurt. June's reply explained that she had wanted a private time for grieving with the children and their families. Back came an even angrier note, which June crumpled and bounced off the wall with a shout of "good riddance to you." Apologizing to the woman was the furthest thing from her mind.

Then over the next few days, a biblical passage kept intruding on her thoughts, "If you have something against your brother, leave your gift at the altar and go make peace." She tried hard to put herself in her sister-in-law's place and feel the pain of rejection that she obviously had felt. Then June decided that, even though there was nothing wrong in wanting to be alone with her family, leaving her sister-in-law out had been insensitive and (truth to tell) had given her a certain malicious pleasure. So she wrote a letter of apology. Her sister-in-law immediately accepted it and suggested they put the matter behind them.

"I forgive you"

We noted in chapter 1 that forgiveness is one of the most fundamental forms of loving kindness. Bringing our minds and hearts to forgive others is only the first difficulty, however. The second is putting our forgiveness into suitable words. The temptation can be great to attach an addendum in the form of a lecture or admonition. Suppose that a friend lied to you about something important and you have known for some time that she did. Suppose, too, that she has just apologized and you have decided to forgive her. In expressing your forgiveness, you may be tempted to say, "I forgive you, *but* I want you to know I was deeply hurt by that lie. I had always trusted you and then, when I found out that you deceived me, I felt betrayed . . . ." And so on. Or you may want to say, "I forgive you now, *but* I'm not sure I could ever forgive you if you lied to me again."

The message conveyed in each of these statements is, "Though I am saying I forgive you, I really don't, at least not completely." Such a message rubs the person's nose in the offense and could easily make him sorry he apologized. A moment's reflection on how difficult it is for *you* to apologize will make you appreciate how delicate the situation is for the other person. Here is a good guide to follow in such circumstances: The only thing that can be safely added to the words "I forgive you" is a handshake or a hug.

"I'll remember you in my prayers"

These words are appropriate whenever someone is troubled over something. For example, whenever he or she has lost a loved one, been diagnosed with a serious illness, been laid off from work, is concerned about a family member, or is having financial or legal problems. Despite the words' appropriateness, however, many people, even very religious people, are reluctant to say them. "What if the person is an agnostic or atheist?" they wonder. "Will she think I am trying to force my religion on her?" Fearful of being misunderstood, they choose to offer the prayer in secret.

In reality, any such risk is far too small to worry about. Saying you will pray for someone is no different from saying, "I think enough of you to ask God to bless you." Generally speaking, even non-religious people will recognize the loving kindness in this.

Never Postpone a Kind Word

Not long ago I lost a good friend to cancer. I had known him for almost fifty years. We had been classmates in college and later taught in the same department at another college. We went to meetings, convocations, and conferences together, and discussed the events of the day in our offices or the faculty lounge. Our families went to the same church and often got together for special events. Then I left the area and lost contact with him.

When I learned of my friend's death, I reflected what a wonderful man he had been; how I had admired him for his willingness to help anyone in need, in ways large and small; and how much I had valued his friendship. I also realized how many opportunities to express these thoughts and feelings I had let slip by. At any one of hundreds of moments, I could have offered a well-deserved and heartfelt compliment—there were innumerable ways to do so without seeming sentimental or "unmanly." Unfortunately, I squandered every one of those moments and the only opportunity left was to tell his widow what I never told him.

How foolish I was. And how foolish you will be if you postpone telling people close to you what you feel about them while you still have the chance.

Trust and Be Patient

Contemporary culture promises and often delivers so much instant gratification that you may tend to expect it of all your efforts, including your expressions of loving kindness. If your words do not produce the desired response right away, you may be tempted to consider them a bad investment. This is a mistake. Unlike angry, hateful words, which produce an immediate response, loving words often require weeks, months, or even longer to take root in people's minds and hearts. We simply must trust that our patience will be rewarded.

Ellen's bachelor great-uncle was suffering from dementia and living in a nursing home. He was often sarcastic, crude, and cynical, and treated visitors, fellow patients, and the staff badly. Yet Ellen visited him faithfully and spoke amiably and cheerfully with him—even after he got angry, swore at her, and told her to go away and stay away. Over a period of months, she slowly gained his trust and broke down the emotional barriers he had erected. Then one day, toward the end of his life, he was lying in his bed, sick with the latest of many bouts of pneumonia. Ellen held his hand and said she loved him, as she had many times before. But this time, unlike the others, he squeezed her hand and whispered, with tears streaming down his cheeks, "I love you, too."

An elderly friend of Lucy's had recently undergone back surgery and was staying in a two-bed hospital room for the early stages of her rehabilitation. The other bed was occupied by a woman who never spoke, moved, or made a noise. From all appearances she was catatonic. Lucy lived near enough to the hospital that she was able to visit her friend every day, and on passing the other woman's bed she would greet her and ask how she was feeling. The woman never returned Lucy's gaze or gave any hint that she heard or understood. This went on for about a week—Lucy speaking, the woman staring off into space, and the friend saying that Lucy was wasting her breath.

Then Lucy was unable to visit her friend for a few days. On her next visit, she had barely entered the room when the "catatonic" woman sat up and said, "Where have you been? I missed you." Amazed at this response, Lucy stayed and talked for a while, this time *with* her rather than *at* her. Over the next several days, the woman seemed to improve more and more. Then one day her bed was empty and Lucy's friend explained that she had improved enough to be discharged.

A similar but even more dramatic example of the value of patience occurred for Tom, a clergyman. Years before I knew him, he had been a chaplain in a mental hospital and one of the patients there was not just apparently but *actually* catatonic. Tom told me that every day when he made his rounds of the patients, he would have a one-way conversation with the man. He would mention the weather, interesting items in the news, conversations he had had with other patients, and any other light topic of conversation that occurred to him. Then he would say a short prayer aloud and continue on his rounds.

These one-way conversations went on for months and Tom eventually felt foolish for spending time with someone who was mentally absent. Nevertheless, he kept visiting and talking. Then one day, unaccountably, the man emerged from his catatonic state and expressed his gratitude. "You'll never know what a consolation it was to me," he explained, "when the doctors and nurses were treating me like a fixture, to have one person treat me as a human being. I heard and understood every word you said and derived great consolation from your visits, even though I was unable to give any indication that I did. Thank you for giving me hope."

Conveying Unpleasant Messages

So far in this chapter, we have considered examples of loving kindness in which the message has been affirming and positive. But it would be a mistake to infer that all disapproval is unkind. If parents learn that their child is engaged in illegal drug use, they should, at the very least, voice their displeasure. If a teacher catches students plagiarizing, he should chastise them and perhaps give them a failing grade for the assignment. If an employee learns that her company is polluting the environment or engaging in criminal fraud, she should report the offense to the appropriate authorities.

Decent people understandably balk at causing someone pain, financial difficulty, embarrassment or, worse, public disgrace and imprisonment. Their first reaction is that doing so would be unkind. The problem with this thinking is that it is too narrowly focused. To report a harasser, burglar, or child molester is, in a sense, unkind to him but wonderfully kind to all his victims. Conversely, *not* reporting the victimizer would be kind to him but unkind to the others. The choice in such cases is between *two kindnesses*, and the decision should be for the greater kindness.[1]

Jim went out to his car one morning, found a small puddle of antifreeze under it, and promptly drove to the service department. The service manager had one of his mechanics inspect the car, then announced gravely that the leaking was coming from the head gasket and the repair would cost nine hundred dollars. Jim was disappointed but he needed the car to get to work, so he made an appointment to have the repair done the following Wednesday. But when he returned home, he stopped to chat with his next door neighbor, who suggested getting a second opinion and recommended a small auto shop. Jim followed his advice and received a very different diag-

---

1. It could, of course, be argued that reporting a wrongdoer represents a kindness even to him. It halts the wrongdoing and helps him redirect his life.

nosis. "It's just a bad radiator hose," the mechanic said, "and I can replace it for forty dollars."

Because Jim was a kind man, he did not confront the service manager; he simply called and canceled his appointment. But later, after thinking about how many other people might be similarly victimized, he decided that their protection was a greater good than the service manager's feelings. So he called the car manufacturer's consumer division and told them his story.

Is it possible to convey an unpleasant or a harsh message in a loving way? Absolutely. As Faustina Kowalska wisely observed, "A severe word flowing from sincere love does not wound the heart."[2] The challenge is to feel sincere benevolence for the person you are speaking to (or about) and to place the severe words in a context of loving kindness.

For example, when a Buddhist Abbot in Thailand discovered that some of his monks had been growing marijuana, he called all the monks together and announced calmly that the guilty monks would have to leave the monastery. He spoke without anger or accusation, even though the offense was serious and had disgraced him as a teacher. Then, as an expression of loving kindness, he sent the monks away with new clothes and some money and encouraged them to continue their search for enlightenment as lay Buddhists. Later, he even supported one monk's petition to enter another monastery.

The same approach can be used in potentially violent situations, as a nightclub bouncer named Larry learned.

---

2. Faustina Kowalska (1905-1938) was a Polish nun whose life was characterized by profound meditation on God's mercy. She was canonized by Pope John Paul II in the year 2000.

Though he tried to practice loving kindness in his personal life, he adopted a different, tougher demeanor on the job—seldom smiling, speaking only to warn someone to behave or to tell him to leave, and regarding everyone as a potential offender. But then he wondered whether loving kindness might be a better way. So he started smiling at people as they entered the club. When they reacted positively and treated him warmly, he began moving from table to table and conversing with people. If someone became boisterous or quarrelsome and he felt it necessary to exercise control, he delivered a gentle "reminder" rather than a warning, in a friendly, even humorous way. This approach, he discovered, was not only more pleasant for him and others but also more effective.

Guidelines for Difficult Situations

As we have seen, it is possible to convey even unpleasant or harsh messages with loving kindness. Here are some simple guidelines for doing so.

Avoid speaking or writing when you are angry. Communicating in anger usually makes the situation worse, producing hurting rather than healing, alienation rather than reconciliation. Whenever you are angry, wisdom suggests you refrain from speaking or writing. And the angrier you are, the longer you should wait. Only when you have calmed yourself and considered various ways of expressing your thoughts will you be likely to speak or write with loving kindness.

Expect a defensive reaction to your words. It is human nature for people to recoil from unpleasant messages, particularly when they concern some personal fault or failing.

Moreover, the more *deserved* the criticism, the greater the inclination to become defensive. You've certainly observed this behavior, not only in others but in yourself. Even so, if you are like most people, you expect others to be gracious and accepting when they receive unpleasant messages from you. If, instead, they try to save face by claiming that the criticism is false and unfair, you are astounded and become angry and defensive yourself. "I try so hard to be loving and kind and what do I get?" you say to yourself, "nothing but abuse."

The way to avoid this descent into self-pity and animosity is to lower your expectations. Tell yourself at the outset that no matter how lovingly you present your criticism, the person's first reaction will almost certainly be resentment and denial. Understand that this reaction is natural and refuse to be offended by it. Instead, be patient and hope that a more honest and rational response will, in time, supplant it.

Remain calm and courteous. If the other person is upset by what you say, emotion may cause her to behave inappropriately. For example, she may raise her voice, interrupt you when you speak, recite a long litany of your faults (real or imagined), and dredge up irrelevant past disputes. Such occasions will test your loving kindness. If you can continue speaking calmly and courteously despite this assault, you will pass the test.

Chapter 4

Loving Kindness in Actions

The scene is Auschwitz, the infamous death camp, in 1941. An inmate has attempted to escape and the Nazis are in the process of exacting a penalty: a group of inmates will be isolated in a cell and starved to death. The commandant of the camp is walking up and down the ranks of prisoners, choosing one victim, then another, until he reaches the specified number. One of the chosen ones begins sobbing aloud, "My wife and my children," but the commandant ignores his plea.

Then suddenly, from the back of the ranks another man pushes his way forward and asks for permission to take the condemned man's place. The commandant asks who he is and the man replies, "A Catholic priest. I have no family. Besides, I'm old and not good for anything. He's in better condition."

The commandant grants the request, the man with the family is spared, and Maximilian Kolbe, the "saint of Auschwitz," is led away to his death.

Our reaction to such stories is a combination of awe and wonder. We rejoice at the human capacity for heroic selflessness and ask ourselves what it takes to be a hero and whether we would ever have the courage to be one.

What Makes a Hero?

Do heroes possess a special gift, an extraordinary capacity for loving kindness beyond that of the average person? It is impossible to say for sure, but this much is certain: Whatever gift or talent they possess requires development. Heroic acts of loving kindness, like great performances in music or in dance, are the culmination of years of training. Look closely at lives of the kindest, most loving people who have walked among us—the Gandhis, the Mother Teresas—and that training becomes evident.

This was certainly the case with Maximilian Kolbe. His life was so filled with acts of loving kindness that no one who knew him was surprised when he gave his life for a stranger. In his youth he asked his mother to "pray that I will love without any limits." As a student he was solicitous of those who were sad or in pain, yet never complained of his own frequent suffering from tuberculosis. Later, as a priest, he treated fellow priests and brothers with extraordinary kindness. When the Nazis threw him into a cattle car bound for Auschwitz, he cheered his companions by leading them in song. In the camp he was a source of comfort and encouragement to the other inmates and often gave away his own meager food ration.

A Jewish man who was thirteen at the time he was imprisoned with Kolbe, recalls of him: "His heart was bigger than persons—that is, whether they were Jewish, Catholic, or whatever. He loved everyone. He dispensed nothing but love."

Begin Modestly

The lesson of Maximilian Kolbe's life is that small acts of love prepare for greater ones in much the same way that running longer and longer distances prepares one to run a marathon. Here are some examples of small acts of loving kindness.

Keep your word. If you say you will meet someone at 7 p.m., make the necessary changes in your schedule to be there exactly on time or even a little early. When you promise to do something, no matter how seemingly inconsequential, keep your word. If, for some reason, you find it impossible (as opposed to merely inconvenient) to do so, find a way to make amends.

Be the first to volunteer for menial or onerous tasks. Around the home such tasks might include washing dishes or clothes, dusting or vacuuming, raking leaves or cleaning the garage. At work, an unwanted committee assignment or an unpopular project. In organizations, making telephone calls or setting up for or cleaning up after an event.

Give away something. Let someone go in front of you in traffic or at the grocery store checkout. Or give away a privilege as six-year-old Jennifer did when she let her brother take her turn riding in the front seat of the car. If you have an item of clothing you don't need, a book you have read, or a piece of furniture you are tired of, give it to a charity such as the Salvation Army, so that someone less fortunate than you can benefit from it. Four-year-old John Sammy sent his favorite stuffed animals to poor children in Romania. (What made this gesture touching was that, at the time, John Sammy was suffering from a rare lung cancer that would claim his life within months.)

Visit a lonely person. Twelve-year-old Francis had a news-paper route after school. The last stop on the route was the trailer home of an elderly widow. Knowing that she lacked company, he made it a point to spend fifteen or twenty minutes talking to her every day. (The fact that she always had some cookies waiting for him did not diminish the generosity of his action.) Undoubtedly, there are at least a few people in your neighborhood who would appreciate a visit from time to time. In addition to the elderly, consider those who are convalescing from illnesses or accidents.

Pass Kindness On

Remember cartoonist Scott Adams' experience with loving kindness? An established cartoonist encouraged him and motivated him to persevere. In reflecting on this experience later, Adams discovered the valuable insight that "some gifts are meant to be passed on, not repaid."

No story illustrates this insight more clearly for me than that of Anthony, a young Italian immigrant to the United States in the 1920s. In those days, a requirement for entry into the country was that one have at least twenty dollars to support himself until he could find work. Anthony had arrived at Ellis Island with only sixteen dollars and would have been sent back to Italy had it not been for the loving kindness of a passing stranger who gave him the extra four dollars.

Anthony was grateful and promised to repay the stranger as soon as he could earn the money, but in the excitement and confusion of the admission process, he never learned the man's name. Subsequently, on a number of occasions, he tried to find the man but could not. Anthony took a railroad station job first in New York City and then in Rochester, where he eventually became the stationmaster. But he never forgot the stranger's kindness and repaid it again and again by practicing loving kindness to those he found in need.

Once, as Anthony was walking through the station, he noticed a woman sitting on a bench. Next to her sat a small child drinking a bottle of milk. The milk was so spoiled that Anthony could smell it as he passed. Inquiring about her circumstances, he learned that she was traveling to a distant city to meet her husband. She had a ticket on a train leaving the next morning but no money for food or lodging. Anthony took her and the child to a restaurant and bought them a meal. Then he took them to a nearby hotel and arranged for their lodging.

On another occasion he noticed a man in a clerical collar staggering through the terminal, reeking of alcohol. Many people would have simply judged the man unworthy of his vocation and walked on. But Anthony asked him where he was going. Though his tongue was thick, the man managed to explain through his tears that his mother had died suddenly and he was traveling to her funeral. Anthony concluded that his drunken state was attributable to grief rather than dissolution, so he removed the clerical collar and put it in the man's pocket. Then he called a cab and told the driver to take the man to a nearby hotel and charge the room to him. (By then local innkeepers were familiar with Anthony's kindness and knew he would pay them.) The next morning the clergyman, sober and ashamed, found Anthony at the train station, reimbursed him, and gave him a special blessing.

Such acts of loving kindness were typical of Anthony, his daughter explained to me, and every one was done in appreciation of that stranger's kindness at Ellis Island. Throughout his life, whenever he spoke of that stranger, his eyes filled with tears of gratitude.

Look for Unmet Needs

Claudia and Joe lived next door to a mentally disturbed elderly woman who was suspicious of everyone. On more than one occasion she accused them of trespassing or cheating her in some way. Claudia, sensing how lonely the woman must have been and speculating that she might not be eating well, decided to prepare a meal for her each day. When the meal was ready, she would put it on a tray on the woman's front porch, then knock on the door and leave, returning later to pick up the tray and the empty dishes. This went on for months until the woman was taken away to a home for the aged.

On the other side of Claudia and Joe lived an elderly couple. Once, the man brought over a single egg and asked Claudia to prepare a custard for his wife, who he said was not feeling well. Claudia wondered whether he realized that it takes many eggs, as well as milk and sugar, to make a custard. But she focused on the need and not the possibly unworthy motive and made the custard. On another occasion, the same man brought over one apple and asked for an apple pie, which she also made. Rather than being offended, she saw the humor in these requests. Before long, she was sending the couple casseroles as well.

All this occurred during the Great Depression, when food and money were scarce, and Claudia's fifteen-year-old daughter was understandably upset with her mother. "Don't you realize they are taking advantage of you? Why don't you just say no?" she would say. Her mother would simply smile and reply, "I don't mind doing it." In time the girl came to understand that her mother was not being taken advantage of at all but seizing opportunities for loving kindness.

It is easy to find unmet needs if we are observant. About two weeks before Christmas, Michele learned that the recently divorced mother across the street was having financial difficulties. So Michele discussed the matter with her husband and teenage children. They decided to put together a food basket, which included a ham, fruit, crackers, and some small gifts for the woman's children.

Val was driving to the store in the aftermath of an ice storm that had knocked out electrical power when he passed a police officer directing traffic at a windblown intersection. "He must be freezing," Val thought, and wondered how he might make the cold night a little more bearable. So on his way back he stopped at a convenience store, bought a large cup of coffee, and gave it to the officer.

When a tropical storm was approaching his Florida coastal town, Bill decided to move his car from his condominium parking lot to higher ground. As he was walking to his car, he passed the cars of two neighbors, both widows in their eighties. "They may be nervous about moving their cars in such windy conditions," he thought. So he got their keys and did it for them.

The late artist Elaine de Kooning is said to have been devoted to meeting the needs of younger artists. She offered them encouragement and advice, gave them supplies they couldn't afford to buy, bought their works to provide them income, and helped them find galleries that would exhibit their work. One of them, recalling the effect of her kindness, said of her, "She inspired you and gave you faith in yourself."

Be Imaginative

A major cause of missed opportunities to show loving kindness in actions is lack of imagination. Suppose you get the idea of taking a lonely friend out for dinner in a fine restaurant but then decide you can't afford to. Instead of abandoning the idea, you can apply a little imagination and make it fit your pocketbook, for example by taking her to a fast food restaurant, making dinner for her yourself, or just treating her to a special dessert.

Regina and three friends were discussing a poor single woman who lived in their neighborhood. She had been an invalid for fourteen years and her house was badly in need of cleaning. They wanted to help but couldn't think of a way because each of them had young children at home. Then Regina came up with a clever solution—one of them would babysit all their children while the other three helped the woman. The plan worked beautifully. They not only cleaned and organized the house, did the laundry, and carted away a lot of trash; after learning that the woman was unable to pay some bills, they called the creditors and persuaded them to relax the payment schedules. Before they left, they prepared lunch for the woman and spent some time talking with her.

In my research for this book, I found many examples of imaginative acts of loving kindness. An old retired gentleman cuts neighbors' lawns and trims their hedges without their knowledge while they are at work. A woman carries items for the homeless in her car, including socks, gloves, toothpaste, and aspirin. A young businessman carries McDonald's meal coupons in his pocket and gives them away to needy people he passes on the street. An elderly man with artistic talent sends postcards with cheerful messages to shut-ins; he decorates each card with sketches of flowers and birds. A woman scans the daily newspaper for stories of unusual kindness or heroism and writes notes of praise and appreciation to the people involved.

One imaginative act of loving kindness that has become famous occurred in the fifteenth century in a small village near Nuremburg. Two brothers showed artistic talent but their parents couldn't pay for their schooling because they had sixteen other children to support. So the boys, Albert and Albrecht Dürer, decided that one of them would go work in the mines and pay for the other to attend school. Four years later, the one who had received schooling would repay the other for his sacrifice.

When Albrecht returned from the academy to keep his promise, however, he learned that Albert's hands had been injured in the mines and were now so badly crippled with arthritis that his dream of becoming an artist would never be realized. So Albrecht found another way to repay him, by creating a work of art that today is better known than any of his other portraits, watercolors, woodcuts, and engravings. No doubt you have seen it, a sketch of his brother's hands, joined in prayer. The masterpiece is known simply as "The Praying Hands."

Be Spontaneous

Not all acts of kindness are carefully thought out in advance. For example, I read of a man who, when the spirit moves him, pays for the stranger behind him in a coffee shop. Another man sometimes buys extra tickets at an amusement park and gives them to the parents of children who appear to be poor. A third will, from time to time, crumple up a dollar bill and drop it on the ground, knowing that whoever picks it up will be pleased.

One of the simplest ways to express loving kindness spontaneously is to compliment others. Opportunities to do this arise every day. For example, if a co-worker's outfit is unusually well coordinated in color and style, or a man's tie "sets off" his suit, tell the person. If you are riding in the elevator admiring someone's purse or briefcase, express your admiration aloud. Similarly, if you are walking in the mall parking lot and someone gets out of a car that you think is attractive, say "That's a beautiful car."

There is a fine but important difference between being spontaneous and being impulsive or impetuous. Being spontaneous means acting quickly and naturally without a lot of pondering or planning but with sensitivity to the people and the situation. This sensitivity will help you avoid acting inappropriately and causing anyone embarrassment.

More Difficult Challenges

If you do nothing more than follow the approaches to loving kindness discussed thus far in this chapter, you will be a true *mensch*, or angel of kindness. However, you can regard these approaches merely as the prelude to acts that require a greater sacrifice of money or time and effort.

Bart worked with a man who was having trouble supporting his wife and three children. The financial difficulties soon became serious enough to cause a strain in the man's marriage. Bart wanted to help the family, so he got a cashier's check for eight hundred dollars and sent it to them anonymously. In a similar case, Ken knew a nurse's aide who was struggling to support herself and her son while completing her studies for a nursing degree, so he sent her a cashier's check for fifteen hundred dollars.

An extraordinary example of monetary generosity occurred in 1995 in a small Massachusetts town. At that time three buildings of the Malden Mills plant, whose principal product is Polartec garments, were destroyed by fire. Many company owners would have been content to take the insurance money and move the company to another state or country where the operating expenses would be considerably lower. But that thought never occurred to Malden Mills' president and owner, Aaron Feuerstein. He not only rebuilt the plant in the same location but kept all thirty-four hundred employees on the payroll during the three months it took for rebuilding. The cost to him personally was an estimated twelve million dollars.

If you can't afford to give hundreds, let alone millions of dollars, you might consider supporting a needy child through one of the many charitable organizations such as Save the Children or Christian Children's Fund. The cost is only sixty or seventy cents a day and payments can be made monthly. For Christmas or the child's birthday you can add a little extra for a present. Nick, a friend of mine, supports a child in India and last Christmas he sent an extra thirty dollars. In her thank-you letter the child specified what she was able to buy with the money: "1 blouse, 1 petticoat, 1 pair of slippers for me, 3 pairs of pants, 1 shirt and 1 pants for my father, 2 pairs of jeans for my brother, and 1 steel water pot for our family's use." All that for thirty dollars!

If you prefer to give time and effort rather than money, consider volunteering for a service organization. There are many such organizations. Some provide mentoring for children from single-parent families. Still others provide food and shelter for the indigent, deliver meals to shut-ins, transport people to hospitals and clinics, or care for the terminally ill.

Many people feel more comfortable performing their acts of loving kindness alone rather than through a formal program. For example, Regina, a banking executive, has developed a special relationship with a boy and girl who have muscular dystrophy. She often takes them to concerts and sporting events. She also spends her vacations accompanying the girl to a special MD camp.

When Bernice and her husband Ralph learned about an eighty-year-old blind man who was recovering from a brain tumor, they put together a food basket and paid him a visit. When they arrived, they found him wandering outside his trailer home, moaning in a low voice for someone to help him find the door. They not only helped him that day, but began visiting him once a week and occasionally taking him to their home to cut his hair, soak his feet, and wash his clothes. When his needs became too great for them to meet by themselves, they put an ad in the local newspaper describing his situation and asking for help. More than fifty people responded.

Remember John Sammy, the four-year-old who while suffering from terminal lung cancer gave his stuffed animals to poor children in Romania? For the last year of his life, his parents, Marie and Ed, drove him to a hospital two hours away for chemotherapy. Each time they went, they saw another cancer patient, fifteen-year-old Margaret. Her thinness and pale complexion was accentuated by her hair loss, and their hearts went out to her. Soon they noticed that no family member was ever there to comfort her through the bouts of nausea that followed chemotherapy. The nurses explained that her parents were divorced and neither seemed interested in her.

So Marie began bringing her cards and small gifts and spending some time with her while Ed stayed with John Sammy. At about the time John Sammy died, Margaret's condition worsened and she was moved to the "terminal ward." Marie, in her grief over the loss of her only child, never wanted to see that hospital again. Yet she forced herself to take the two-hour drive twice a week to visit Margaret.

What made the experience even more difficult for Marie was the fact that Margaret was becoming bitter. She felt abandoned not only by her parents but by God as well. "Why is God making me die?" she would ask. Marie's own religious faith was still strong despite being tested during John Sammy's suffering. But she simply responded, "I don't have all the answers about life and death" and held Margaret's hand. Eventually, Margaret asked Marie to read the Bible to her and pray with her and Marie obliged. Margaret died soon, shortly after her sixteenth birthday. The only people at her funeral were Marie, Ed, and several nurses.

At this point, Marie and Ed could have vowed never again to visit a cancer ward voluntarily and, if possible, to avoid contact with cancer patients. After all, seeing other people suffering would be a vivid reminder of all that their little boy had gone through. Eventually, however, parents who had lost children to cancer and other diseases began to contact them and ask for advice on coping with their grief. Marie and Ed couldn't refuse to help. Today such counseling has become their life's work. The painful memories it evokes are more than compensated by the consolation they get from meeting others' needs.[1] They also understand more deeply the truth of the proverb, "God draws good from evil."

Marie and Ed's situation is not as unusual as you might think. The experience of grief or compassion has led many people to extraordinary expressions of loving kindness, some of them with global impact . After Karen Graham lost her twenty-one-year-old son Billy to skin cancer, she founded the William S. Graham Foundation for Melanoma Research to raise public awareness of the condition and fund research initiatives. After Cindi Lamb and Candace Lightner lost their daughters in (separate) accidents, they joined forces and formed Mothers Against Drunk Driving (MADD). The organization, which has hundreds of chapters in the United States and other countries, conducts educational programs, supports government policy and legislation, and provides victim assistance.

Millard Fuller was a self-made millionaire at age twenty-nine but then experienced health and marital problems. In response to these challenges, he and his wife sold all their possessions and looked for a way to serve the poor, eventually founding Habitat for Humanity, which has built more than one hundred thousand homes for low income families.

---

1. Marie and Ed have found that one of the first questions people who have lost a child ask of a counselor is, "Have *you* ever lost a child?" Only when the answer is affirmative do they seem comfortable receiving counsel.

Craig Kielburger, age twelve, was looking for the comic section of the newspaper when he noticed an article about a Pakistani child who had been sold into bondage, escaped, and finally was murdered for speaking out against his captors. Outraged by the story, Craig and several of his friends started Free the Children, an organization that calls attention to the plight of young children forced into slave labor.

Accept the Challenges Life Poses

Often there is no need to seek greater challenges to loving kindness because life brings them to you. Agnes is one of six children but, unlike her brothers and sisters, is unmarried. Several years ago, it became clear that her elderly parents could no longer live alone, and Agnes was the logical choice to be caregiver. She accepted the responsibility without complaining, gave up her apartment, and moved in with her parents. Now, before leaving for work each day, she makes their breakfast and lunch and lays out their medications. After work, she makes their dinner. She also accompanies them to the doctor's office and takes them shopping.

A good number of grandparents have taken the responsibility for raising their grandchildren when drug and alcohol problems have rendered their children unable to be good parents. And many men and women are caring for spouses with physically or mentally crippling diseases. One of the most moving examples I have seen of loving kindness was just such a case.

About five years ago my wife and I noticed an elderly couple walking around the marina that borders our condominium; her gait and manner suggested that she was in the early stages of Alzheimer's disease. A week or so later, when we saw them walking around the condominium grounds, we realized that they lived in a neighboring building. Over the next few months we saw them regularly on the grounds, in a nearby park, at the grocery store, and in church.

The woman's ability to function declined noticeably over the next few years, yet her husband's attentiveness never diminished. If anything, it increased! Although he cared for her by himself, her hair was always combed and her clothing was always neat, clean, and attractive. Day in and day out, he took her out into the community, always content to walk at her measured pace, stopping to sit whenever she wanted or needed to. Whenever the condominium had a social event, he brought her and remained by her side. Recently, we began to see him alone and learned that his wife had to be placed in a nursing home, where we understand he visits her every day.

Never once over the last five years did my wife and I see that elderly gentleman display the slightest sign of impatience or unkindness toward his wife. His patience was limitless, his gentleness constant, his example of selfless love inspiring.

Chapter 5

Loving Kindness in Silence

My mother and father divorced when I was nine, and I lived with her for a time in New York City. Eventually, however, my father learned that she was not properly caring for me and gained custody. Subsequently, I was raised by his partner's family in the Catskill Mountains. However, I maintained contact with my mother during my school and college years, exchanging letters with her and occasionally visiting her. In 1957 she attended my wedding and a year later visited me to see her new granddaughter for the first time. On that occasion, unfortunately, she attempted to sow discord between my wife and me. Having seen her behave similarly in the past, I took her aside and asked her to promise to respect my marriage. She refused to do so and broke off all contact with me.

One Sunday morning in 1996, *thirty-eight years later*, I was reading in my Florida home. Suddenly, a silent command appeared in my mind: "Find your mother." Since I never address myself in the third person, I took it as a message from God and did not hesitate to obey. The only problem was, I had no idea where my mother was or even if she was still alive. By then she would have been in her mid-eighties. Why was I being directed to find her? I wondered. Would she die soon? Would I?

The more pressing question was how to conduct my search. Should I start in New York City, where she had lived for most of her life? Might she be in another state, or perhaps in Canada where she had been born and raised? She had numerous sisters, but they were quite a bit older than she and even if they were alive, I had no idea where they might be. Taking a chance, I checked for my cousin's name in the Maryland directory. Fortunately, he still lived in the town he had moved to as a small child. I asked about his mother and father (both dead), our aunts (all dead) and then—holding my breath—about my mother. "I think she's living in Florida," he explained. I asked him where: Miami? Orlando? Tallahassee? He had no idea.

Accordingly, I decided to begin my search in my local telephone directory. There was no need to look further. *She was living three miles away and had been there for twenty-two years.*

I found it difficult to believe. When I had retired from teaching six years earlier, I had considered moving to any one of half a dozen states. Yet I had not only chosen the state she was living in, but a location almost within walking distance of her home! The odds of that happening by chance were about the same as those of a three-legged horse winning the Kentucky Derby. But the way I had been directed to find her had already convinced me this was not a matter of chance.

I called her right away. We were both understandably cautious, so the conversation was strained at first; but with thirty-eight years of information to exchange, it soon became comfortable. In the course of that discussion, I thanked her for giving me the gift of life and forgave her for neglecting me as a child. My last words were "I love you."

From that moment on, we were together often. Within a year, however, she was diagnosed with lung cancer and six months later she died. Through all those months we talked about many things, yet she never mentioned our past relationship. Nor did she ever say that she loved me.

Sparing Others Discomfort

Why my mother remained silent puzzled me. She had always had unusually facility with words and that skill was still evident then. For example, when a fall put her into the hospital for a brief time, a social worker asked her some simple questions to evaluate her mental capacity. To the question "What is the most beautiful thing you've ever seen?" my mother replied, "the Aurora Borealis," and launched into a vivid description of that phenomenon.

Every time we were together during those last eighteen months, I wanted to ask a host of questions. Had she loved me as a child? If so, why had she neglected me? Why did she find my request for civility so unacceptable that she broke off our relationship? Did she wonder about me during our long estrangement? Did she miss me? What did she feel toward me now? And most of all, why was she reluctant to speak of these matters? The answers, I believed, would help me know her and myself better. Nevertheless, I decided that the most appropriate response to her silence was to be silent myself, so I never asked my questions.

After my mother died, I gained an insight of sorts. At her funeral one of her friends explained that the day before her death, she had grasped that friend's hand (an uncharacteristic gesture) and said, "You know, I really do care, but I have trouble expressing it." Perhaps she really had always loved me and couldn't bring herself to say so. Then again, perhaps she did not love me, at least not until recently, and her silence was intended to spare me the pain of knowing. Of one thing I was certain, my silence had been a kindness to her.

Remember Anthony, the young immigrant who was so grateful for the four dollars he received from a stranger that he spent the rest of his life repaying it? One of his most admirable expressions of loving kindness was made in silence. Before he had left Italy, a teacher had told him he was exceptionally bright and should continue his education. After taking up residence in the United States, he worked hard at not one but three jobs, saving every dollar he could so that he could go to college. However, just when he had accumulated enough to begin his studies, his elder brother became gravely ill. Anthony hired a full-time nurse for him, and by the time his brother succumbed, all the education money had been spent. Yet he never let his brother know of his sacrifice.

Martha is a high school teacher. One day while she was teaching a class, the school librarian burst into her room and began a tirade of accusations, accusing Martha of removing a numbered textbook without recording the name of the student who received it. She further demanded that Martha provide the required information to her by 2 p.m. that same day. Martha was offended, not only because the tirade had occurred in front of her students, but because the accusation was false. Yet, before she responded, she tried to put herself in the librarian's place and thought, "How difficult it must be to be responsible for all the books for eighteen hundred students, and how frustrating to have others upset the system."

That thought enabled Martha to hold back the angry response she was tempted to make. Instead, she promised the librarian she would provide the information by the requested time. Between classes Martha learned that a coach had taken the book for a football player who was in the hospital. She then called the hospital, got the book's number, and delivered it before 2 p.m. When the librarian snatched the sheet from her hand and gave her a hostile look, Martha remained silent. During the next period, however, her silent kindness was rewarded with a handwritten note of apology from the librarian.

Viktor Frankl, the psychiatrist who spent years in Nazi concentration camps, recounts an inspiring example of loving kindness in silence. In this case, the silence did more than spare someone discomfort. It saved a life. One of Frankl's fellow inmates, driven by hunger, had broken into the potato storehouse and stolen a few pounds of potatoes. When the camp authorities realized the theft had occurred, they ordered the inmates to reveal the guilty person's identity or face a severe punishment—the whole camp would receive no food for an entire day. Though the other inmates knew the man's identify, all twenty-five hundred of them chose to suffer rather than give him up.

Keeping Confidences

Another way to express loving kindness through silence is to keep secret what others have confided in you. When someone explicitly directs you to treat information as confidential, you have an obligation to honor that request.[1] But even if you are not specifically bound to secrecy, it is an act of loving kindness to bind *yourself* to silence. This can be difficult at times. Some people have a way of wheedling information from others. They tease, cajole, plead, and try to make you feel guilty. For example, they may say, "I always share information with you; you should do so with me," or "Trust me. I won't say a word." Or they will engage you in a process of elimination, which goes like this:

Other Person: You know something you aren't saying, I can tell.

You: I can't talk about it.

Other Person: All right, then, just answer this: Is it about Sally or Amy? Does it concern work or something personal? Her husband or her children?

There is no way for you to win the elimination maneuver. Anything you say, such as "It's about Sally" or "It's something personal," narrows the possibilities. One bit of information leads to another. And the more you provide, the greater your betrayal.

Whenever someone asks you about something you are holding in confidence, politely refuse to answer. Just say "I know you wouldn't want me to talk about your business with other people, so I'm sure you understand that I can't talk to you about theirs." If the person persists, smile and change the subject.

---

1. In certain cases, of course, other priorities might take precedence. If someone told you that he committed a crime, you would usually be right in notifying the authorities.

Preserving Reputations

Silence is also the best response to the gossiping impulse. Wherever two or more gossips are gathered, that impulse is sure to be lurking and, for some reason, the worse the tale, the greater the urge to tell it. Most of us are quicker to tell about others' offenses than about their acts of kindness. When someone treats us well, for example, we may take no special notice of the fact; nor are we likely to report the fact to others because we expect to be treated that way. On the other hand, if someone treats us badly, we may be tempted to get on the phone and complain to half a dozen people, "You won't believe what Edna just did to me!"

Even conversations that start out positive and constructive have a way of degenerating into gossip. Let's say you are driving home from a party with someone. You may begin by remarking on the host's good taste in furniture or on the delightful sense of humor of one of the guests. But the discussion may then turn to the faults, failings, and shortcomings of the other guests and even of the host. The same conversational pattern often occurs after a business meeting, a holiday gathering with your family or even, alas, a church service.

Loving kindness calls for as much care in dealing with other people's reputations as with your own. In practical terms, this means never sharing damaging information about other people unless there is a good reason for doing so. If you have solid evidence that a youth counselor has behaved improperly with his charges, by all means report that evidence to the authorities. If a friend says she is thinking about having a particular stock broker handle her investments and you know the broker to be dishonest or incompetent, warn her. But if your only reason for undermining someone's reputation is to gossip, remain silent. In all such cases, the childhood lesson remains a reliable guide: "If you can't say something nice, say nothing at all."

Calming Tense Situations

Silence is also the most prudent response when one or both parties to a situation are so angry or upset that words are likely to make matters worse. Piyapañño, a Buddhist monk from Australia told me of a personal experience of this kind.

The monastery was expecting a weekend visit from a number of government dignitaries and Piyapañño was in charge of preparations. When he called the company that would provide the chairs, he asked for the very best, explaining that the occasion was special. Unfortunately, when the chairs arrived on Friday afternoon, they were filthy and unstable. Piyapañño reported this to the company and was assured that a truckload of replacement chairs would be dispatched at once.

When the truck arrived, the crew leader, who evidently had been called away from his favorite pub, was livid. Already drunk, he leaped from the truck, fists clenched and a stream of obscenities spewing from his mouth. "Where's the bloke in charge?" he demanded. Piyapañño responded gently, "I'm the one in charge." The crew leader came up and put his fist in front of Piyapañño's face, looking for the slightest reason to lash out. Meanwhile, Piyapañño stood silently, arms at his side, and concentrated on feeling loving kindness toward the aggressor. After a moment, the crew leader's anger dissolved and the other monks stepped forward to help the crew unload the chairs.

Will silence always defuse a tense situation? Probably not, but it certainly has a better chance of doing so than anger and insults. Just be sure your silence is not petulant or disdainful, but genuinely loving. If the other person is upset, focus on this thought: *The person before me is not in control of his emotions. My calm will quiet his turbulence; my silence will smother the fire of his words. I choose this response not for my sake but for his.* If you are the one who is upset, just remind yourself of all the times when your emotions caused you to say things you didn't mean and later regretted. Then, for your own sake and the other person's, choose silence.

When Words Fail

So far we have considered situations in which it is prudent to choose silence over words. Let us now consider situations in which there is, in effect, no choice at all because words cannot do justice to your thoughts or feelings. This is often the case with historic injustices or acts of inhumanity.

When the Dalai Lama visited the Nazi concentration camp at Auschwitz, his reaction to the ovens in which innocent people had been cremated was "total revulsion." As he surveyed the displays in the museum, he was struck with the horrible scale of the lack of feeling and the cruelty. He thought of the vulnerability of the very young and very old victims, and of their innocence. No doubt he would have liked to express his sadness to those who suffered there and to console their descendants. But the victims were long gone and their children and grandchildren widely dispersed. So he held his sorrow in silence, praying that such a scourge would never occur again and that he himself "might never contribute to such a calamity."

The institution of slavery prompts similar feelings. To wrench people from their families and villages, put them in chains, and transport them to foreign lands to live little better than horses and oxen, and to perform similar functions, is barbaric. Yet it happened, indeed is still happening in some parts of the world. You may, appropriately, feel anger and deep sorrow over this fact. You also feel a vague sense of guilt, even if neither you nor your ancestors ever victimized others in this way. Yet what words would express these feelings adequately, and to whom would you express them? Like the Dalai Lama, you can only resolve to treat everyone you encounter with loving kindness.

Consider, too, how unfairly men have treated women in many times and places. In this regard, I have always been moved by a poem I first read in college. It was written by John Masefield and is entitled "C. L. M.," the initials of his mother, Caroline Louisa Masefield, who died when he was a child:[2]

> In the dark womb where I began
> My Mother's life made me a man.
> Through all the months of human birth
> Her beauty fed my common earth.
> I cannot see, nor breathe, nor stir,
> But through the death of some of her.

---

2. Reprinted by permission of The Society of Authors as the Literary Representative of the Estate of John Masefield, London.

Down in the darkness of the grave
She cannot see the life she gave.
For all her love, she cannot tell
Whether I use it ill or well,
Nor knock at dusty doors to find
Her beauty dusty in the mind.

If the grave's gates could be undone,
She would not know her little son,
I am so grown. If we should meet
She would pass by me in the street,
Unless my soul's face let her see
My sense of what she did for me.

What have I done to keep in mind
My debt to her and womankind?
What woman's happier life repays
Her for those months of wretched days?
For all my mouthless body leeched
Ere Birth's releasing hell was reached?

What have I done, or tried, or said
In thanks to that dear woman dead?
Men triumph over women still,
Men trample women's rights at will,
And man's lust roves the world untamed.
O grave, keep shut lest I be shamed.

Whenever I read this poem, I feel the need to apologize
for all the wrongs that have been done to women. Many
other men, I suspect, experience a similar urge. However,
no individual can apologize meaningfully for what others
have done; and no general apology can cover innumerable
particular offenses. The best and most meaningful

response a man can have to such emotions is to let them govern his relationships with women.

The Value of Listening

Noticing that a colleague at work seemed very upset, Laura asked if she would like to join her in a break. The woman agreed, so Laura bought her a soda, and they sat down together. Almost immediately, the woman began to describe a problem she was struggling with. Laura said nothing but listened attentively. When the break was finished, they returned to work. Then, a few hours later, as Laura was passing the woman's desk, she asked how she was doing. Smiling, the woman replied, "I feel much better after our talk."

This story contains a pair of morals: We don't need to say a word to be considered great conversationalists; and listening attentively to others can be therapeutic for them. Everyone has a story to tell and the sadder the story, the greater the need to tell it. A woman who runs a homeless shelter says that the most precious thing to many of the people who visit is neither the hot meal nor the cot but the chance to talk to someone who cares enough to listen.

Of course, some people are chatterboxes and others meander around a subject, so much of what we hear may seem insignificant and boring. After listening a short time, we may yearn to hear the sound of our own voice. Still, unless the counsel we intend to offer is unusually insightful *and* we receive an unambiguous signal that the person wants us to speak, remaining silent is the better option. More often than not, the person may talk her way out of her problem and into a solution.

Improved listening is the solution to many family problems. When Sue's son and daughter became teenagers, she began offering unsolicited advice about how they should study, choose friends, do their household chores, and so on. In addition, she often criticized her husband for spending too much time at work and other perceived shortcomings. Then one day it occurred to her that the most needed change in her family was not in her children or in her husband but in herself. She immediately resolved to talk less, listen more, and see things from the other person's perspective. Rather than complain about something left undone, she did it herself, silently. Soon the children and her husband became less defensive and the joy that had characterized their family life in years past began to return.

The same approach can be used to solve problems in business. When Doris was asked to replace someone as chairperson of a committee in her company, she quickly understood why her predecessor had given up the assignment. The group was composed of fifteen people, each representing a large constituency and equipped with a generous supply of ego, pride, and in some cases, arrogance. Predictably, everyone wanted to talk and no one was willing to listen, so arguing, shouting, and exchanging insults were the order of the day.

Doris wondered how to apply loving kindness to that situation. The first and most important step, she decided, was to listen hard enough to penetrate the histrionics. By doing so she came to understand that the most outspoken and abrasive person on the committee was also the most deeply committed, so she sought her out privately and won her confidence. Then at the next committee meeting Doris took charge and acted as "translator," laying out the issues and concerns as they had been explained to her and encouraging polite discourse. As if by magic, the atmosphere changed and committee members became more respectful of one another. This new spirit of cooperation enabled them to reach consensus on the issues, develop a plan, and implement it. Even more impressive, the committee never returned to its raucous, unproductive ways thereafter.

Attentive listening is not only, in itself, an expression of loving kindness. It is also a way of enhancing the other uses of silence discussed throughout this chapter.

Chapter 6

Obstacles to Loving Kindness

In chapter 1 we noted the curious fact that, although loving kindness is universally endorsed in theory, it is widely ignored in practice. The reason for this, as we saw, is that we are an imperfect species. Our knowledge is never complete; our perception and memory are subject to distortion; our judgment is susceptible to error; and our will to act wisely and well is, at best, inconstant.

To acknowledge human imperfection is not in any way to suggest that we are a *worthless* species. Our achievements in science, art, philosophy, government, medicine, technology, and every other aspect of life are too numerous and far-reaching to permit such a notion. No, to say we are imperfect means only that we are less than we could be and, in our most noble moments, want to be. Simply said, every human being is *a work in progress*.

The obvious consequences of human imperfection are particular mistakes in thought, word, and deed. The more subtle consequences are the beliefs, habits, and attitudes that develop from those mistakes. The subtle ones are more problematic not only because they are more difficult to identify, but also because they are more deeply rooted and pose greater obstacles to the practice of loving kindness. C. S. Lewis no doubt had such obstacles in mind when he wrote, "No man knows how bad he is till he has tried very hard to be good." Let us examine the most significant of those obstacles, beginning with the one that is central to our age.

Preoccupation with Self

No concept has received more attention in popular psychology over the last fifty years than the concept of *self*. Given that thousands of books, articles, and tapes have been produced, you might assume that the basic concept is perfectly clear. Unfortunately, that is not the case.

The word "self" is sometimes used to mean unique identity. In this sense, your "self" is something you were, are, and will continue to be—your essential, unchangeable being. Authors who advise you to "accept yourself" generally have this sense of "self" in mind. That is reasonable enough; it would be pointless trying to change what cannot be changed. But the writers don't stop there; they also exhort you to "esteem yourself." What is puzzling about this, and what they never bother to explain, is *why you should admire yourself for being what you just happen to be*.

Adding to the confusion, other writers use the word "self" to mean the *very opposite* of unique identity. To them "self" is a shadow without substance, something that does not yet exist but must be "actualized." The term "self-actualization" is associated with Abraham Maslow, but Carl Rogers advanced a similar notion in his book *Becoming a Person*. Yet there is a serious problem with this idea. If you are a self or a person only after you make yourself one, exactly what were you *before* you accomplished that feat? A non-self or non-person? But how can *nothing*—the absence of anything—make itself into *something*?

A possible explanation is that you are two selves—one a kind of midwife to the other. However, this raises equally perplexing questions. What happens to your first self when the second appears? More importantly, why doesn't the first self simply accept itself and save the effort of becoming something different?[1]

Despite these difficulties and inconsistencies, self-actualization and self-esteem have become dominant themes of every agency of modern culture, including entertainment, advertising, and even education. Unfortunately, those themes tend to produce self-absorption and thus hinder the concern for other people's feelings, needs, and rights that is fundamental to the practice of loving kindness.[2] If you have been influenced by them, as most of us have, you would do well to think less of yourself and more of others. You may wish to go even further and adopt the perspective expressed in the Buddhist proverb, "He, indeed, is the noblest victor who has *conquered* himself."

The wisdom of focusing on others rather than self is also emphasized in the Jewish rabbinical tradition, as illustrated in a tale attributed to Rebbe Levi Yitzchak of Berditchev. A man died and was shown both hell and

---

1. Believe it or not, the muddle sometimes gets worse. Some self literature claims that self-esteem is necessary before self-actualization can occur. In other words, the shadowy self *that doesn't yet exist* must feel good about itself (*what* self?) in order to exist.

2. On a related note, Matthew Henry Buckham has described a gentleman or gentlewoman as "one who thinks more of other people's feelings than his [or her] own rights; and more of other people's rights than his [or her] own feelings."

heaven. In hell he observed many people seated at both sides of a long table with a meal set before them, but each was equipped with a spoon much too long to fit into his or her mouth. As a result, everyone was starving. In heaven the man saw the identical scene, but everyone was well nourished because each was using the long spoon to feed the person across the table.

Mine-Is-Better Attitude

Early in life each of us acquires a mine-is-better attitude, which leads us to assess our Mommy as prettiest, our Daddy as strongest, our tricycle as fastest, our stuffed animal as cuddliest. All such assessments convey the same core message: "Whatever I think, feel, own, or am associated with has special value *because I am special*."[3]

Although we eventually realize that everyone else has the same mine-is-better attitude, we never fully believe that anyone else's claim to it is as legitimate as our own. Thus we never completely outgrow the attitude but merely transfer it from our parents and toys to our political parties, nations, churches, social organizations, racial and ethnic groups and, most importantly, to our thoughts and feelings. For the sake of etiquette or political correctness, we also learn to disguise it, in extreme cases even from ourselves.

How does a mine-is-better attitude impede loving kindness? If we feel our opinions possess an insight lacking in other people's opinions, we are likely to deny them the courtesy of considering theirs. If we secretly believe that

3. The existence of this attitude provides further evidence that most people's sense of self-importance is not at all underdeveloped.

no one has any business disagreeing with us, we will surely
be unkind with those who do so. If we believe that only
our church, political party, nation, racial or ethnic group,
or organization is worthy, we are bound to look down on
all others and disrespect the people associated with them.

The mine-is-better attitude is too much a part of
human nature to be eliminated, but we can learn to
control it and thereby overcome its effects. This does not
mean abandoning our convictions and loyalties,
assuming they were conscientiously formed. Nor does it
mean that we should become relativists and regard all
opinions, entities and organizations as equally good, or
good in the same way. That would be foolish—ideas, like
everything else that human beings produce, are less than
perfect and some are more flawed than others. No,
controlling our mine-is-better attitude means carrying
our convictions and loyalties with humility—that is,
admitting that some of our convictions could be mistaken
or some loyalties misplaced, and then having the courage
to find out whether that is the case.

Overemphasis on Differences

Not long ago I saw a television documentary about a
primitive tribe that lives in the South American jungle. In
the beginning, as the anthropologists and their transla-
tors crossed a clearing, several members of the tribe
stepped cautiously from the jungle. When these individuals were asked who they were, one man kept repeating in
their tribal language, with great emphasis, "I am a human
being." The tribe's humanity may not have been in doubt,
but their differences from the Europeans they were

speaking to, and I am sure from most of the television audience, were apparent.

It soon developed that one of the men of the tribe had received a message that his brother, who lived several days down river, was in danger. Before the man could travel there, he had to find a tree, cut it down, and fashion it into a canoe using a primitive ax. This took him several days. Then, because the finished canoe was too heavy for him to carry several miles to the river, he had to get help. This he did much as you or I might. He shouted to the men and women in his village to come and help him. They did as he asked, quite good-naturedly.

When the man arrived at his brother's little settlement down river, he was relieved to find that the danger had passed. He and his brother embraced and chatted excitedly. "It's been so long. . . . You look well. . . . Remember when we were last together how we ate, drank, and told stories. . . ." Then they joined the other men and women to eat and drink, exchange news and recall past events. This went on for a day or two, until the man took his leave, paddling away from the settlement to a chorus of well-wishing and invitations to return soon.

In the course of that documentary, I came to see those tribespeople not merely as human beings but as neighbors who, by chance, happen to live in very different circumstances than I. The vast gulf between us had been narrowed; the differences that seemed so substantial at the beginning of the show had become insignificant compared to the similarities between us.

My experience is perhaps best explained by the Tibetan concept, *nying je*, which refers to the capacity for empathy that produces a feeling of connectedness. It is not necessary to wait for this feeling to arise by chance, as it did in

my case. It can be stimulated through reflection and practice. This, in fact, is how the Dalai Lama gained his
unusual ability to relate instantly to people of different
cultures, religions, and perspectives. On first meeting
such a person, he says that he feels he is "simply encoun-
tering a fellow human being with the same desire to be
happy and to avoid suffering as myself."[4]

Nying je provides a much needed balance to our current
emphasis on diversity. The idea behind the diversity
movement is that the celebration of racial, cultural, and
ethnic differences will promote understanding and heal
divisions. It is a noble idea, but it tends to ignore the
mine-is-better attitude that disposes us to see what is
different from us as inferior. The divisions among people
are much more likely to be healed by appreciating how *like
us* other people are than how *different* they are. The sense
of unity and brotherhood that follows such appreciation
fosters loving kindness, as the following cases illustrate.

When Pamela transferred to another high school, she
immediately noted that the students were very clannish.
There were a variety of ethnic and racial groups and more
than a little tension among them. Pamela was disappointed in the situation, so she set out to change it. She
befriended a few individuals in different groups and then
decided to try something more ambitious. When a school
project was announced, she persuaded a number of individuals from the various groups to participate, thus
sowing seeds of unity and improving relationships among
the groups.

---

4. The literal meaning of *nying je*, according to the Dalai Lama, is
   compassion, but the term also denotes "love, affection, kindness,
   gentleness, generosity of spirit, and warm-heartedness."

Brent, an executive in a computer company, observed that an *us versus them* mentality existed between the hardware and the software divisions. Each kept to itself except when forced to work together, and then when anything went wrong, each division blamed the other. Brent began bringing selected members of the divisions together for discussions outside the pressure-filled realm of projects so that inter-group relationships could develop. The results were an improved work atmosphere and a greater spirit of teamwork.

The point is not to ignore the differences between various groups but to look beyond them to the underlying similarities, the most basic of which is our common humanity.

Undisciplined Emotion

It is fashionable to believe that the heart is wiser than the mind and that feelings are more trustworthy than reason and logic. According to this view, emotion should be given free expression. Many ancient traditions, however, held the opposite view. An ancient Indian writer compared indulging one's senses to drinking salt water. "The more we partake," he wrote, "the more our desire and thirst grow." The ancient Greeks compared emotion to a wild stallion that will run away with us unless we reign him in. Others have likened it to a fire that, if untended, quickly rages out of control.

The idea that emotion needs to be disciplined is not given much attention in contemporary culture, but it still has many adherents. The Dalai Lama, for example, compares emotion to an elephant. "If left to blunder around out of control," he writes, "it will wreak havoc.

But the harm and suffering we encounter as a result of failing to restrain the negative impulses of mankind far exceed the damage a rampaging elephant can cause. Not only are these impulses capable of bringing about the destruction of things, they can also be the cause of lasting pain to others and to ourselves."

Everyday experience supports this view. Although feelings occasionally prompt us to devote ourselves to our loved ones, help a needy neighbor, or mend a broken relationship, they often cause us to lie, cheat, steal, poison our minds and bodies, yell at our loved ones, and kick the cat. Tibetans call the latter impulses *nyong mong*, "afflictive emotions." The only way to prevent them from hurting us and the people around us is to take control of them.

How should we go about disciplining our emotions? By testing them before we follow them. Ask yourself "Is what I am feeling about this person or situation a healthy feeling? Is it helping me respect myself and others? Is it consistent with the ideal of loving kindness?" Whenever the answer is no, resist the feeling and make an effort to behave as you know you should. C. S. Lewis offers a simple example of this approach: "When you are not feeling particularly friendly . . . the best thing you can do, very often, is to put on a friendly manner and behave as if you were a nicer person than you actually are. And in a few minutes . . . you will be really feeling friendlier than you were."

Face Saving

One of the keys to growing in loving kindness is acknowledging your past lapses and taking steps to avoid them in the future. Face saving occurs when you are more concerned about preserving your self-image than in improving yourself. The most common types of face saving are:

Making excuses. One example is the expression, "That's the way I am," which implies that the speaker's behavior is outside his or her control. The real meaning of this expression is, "You'd better accept me as I am because I have no intention of changing." Another common excuse takes the form of a rhetorical question: "What else could I have done?" The implication here is that no kinder, more loving way of speaking or acting was possible. That is seldom the case.

Minimizing the effects. We often hear people say, "It really wasn't that big a deal" or "He's making a mountain out of a molehill." They may, for example, have borrowed an item of clothing and returned it soiled, broken a promise to someone, or caused another person embarrassment. But *saying* that something is of little consequence doesn't make it so, particularly to the offended person. Moreover, repeated small offenses can have the same effect as one big one.

Shifting responsibility. This form of face saving is an attempt to change the issue from the offense to some alleged deficiency or fault of the offended person. If someone objects to being treated insensitively or cruelly, for example, the offender may say, "You don't have a sense of humor" or "You deserved what you got." In some cases, the offender will raise questions about the offended person's *motive* in complaining. In reality, the responsibility for any offense lies with the offender.

The antidote to these face-saving maneuvers is to adopt the perspective suggested by this ancient Chinese prayer:

"O Lord, convert the world, and begin with me." Seen from this perspective, shortcomings are steppingstones to growth and people who point them out are our benefactors.

Zeal for a Cause or Belief

What do environmentalists, feminists, pacifists, multiculturalists, vegetarians, practitioners of homeopathic medicine, and followers of some religions tend to have in common? Enthusiasm for their cause or belief and the urge to share it with others. In a word, zeal.

Enthusiasts believe that their cause or belief will make people healthier or happier in this life or, in the case of religion, both now and throughout eternity. They also reason that sharing their convictions with others and exhorting them to embrace the cause or belief is an expression of loving kindness. Often as not, however, the recipients of the enthusiasts' zeal regard it as an unneighborly imposition and take offense. And the enthusiasts are left lamenting the hardness of people's hearts.

Some people leap to the conclusion that if expressing convictions can cause hurt feelings, we should avoid having convictions. This reasoning is flawed. The purpose of the human mind is to sort out sense from nonsense, apply reason to facts, reach conclusions, and then embrace them. To put it more succinctly, *the purpose of the human mind is to produce convictions.* Moreover, since all humans live in the same world and are immersed in the same reality, convictions are more appropriately shared than hoarded. This view may be disputed in theory but it is universally accepted in practice. When breakthroughs in understanding occur in any field, the discoverers don't hide their findings. They either take to the streets and shout the fact to their neighbors or do the modern equivalent—hire an agent and call a news conference.

These facts suggest that zeal for convictions is a good thing, even though human imperfection can cause it to be misplaced. Thus when people are offended by someone's zeal, the problem may lie less in the zeal itself than in the manner or form of its expression. What, then, is the right way to express your convictions to others? How can you ensure that your enthusiasm for your cause or belief will be an expression of loving kindness and not an obstacle to it? A partial answer is hinted at in a story told about Francis of Assisi.

One day Francis said to a fellow friar, "Let's go into town and preach," so off they went together, the friar assuming that they would go to the village church, or perhaps the marketplace, and deliver a stirring homily on the teachings of Jesus. As they walked through Assisi, Francis greeted everyone he met and exchanged kind words. When they had walked through the entire town, they retraced their steps and headed home. Just before they reached their destination, the friar, puzzled, said to Francis, "I thought we were going to preach." Francis smiled and said, "We just did."

The lesson of this story is that telling people about your convictions is not the only way to share them. An even more powerful way is to *demonstrate* them in the way you live. If you believe that Jesus is the Son of God, worship him and live in accordance with the Gospel message. If you are convinced that Mohammed is the prophet of Allah, observe the principles set forth in the Q'uran. In such cases, your example will speak more eloquently than words ever could.

This is not to suggest that you should never speak about your convictions. Talking, though never a substitute for demonstration, is an excellent complement to it. As long as you speak with humility and respect for the other person, you need not worry about your zeal for your convictions becoming an obstacle to loving kindness.

Unfortunately, many enthusiasts act as if anyone who does not share their convictions is a simpleton. This is a particular danger in the case of religious enthusiasts, who sometimes assume that people of other faiths have never heard of God and morality. In such cases, they completely ignore the possibility that the people they are trying to "bring to God" may already be as close to God as they are or, perhaps, even closer.

To avoid disrespecting others, get to know them and their views before you unleash your enthusiasm for your cause or belief. This requires attentive listening, genuine interest, and the willingness to embrace insights other than your own. All three practices are unmistakable expressions of loving kindness.[5]

Another way to keep your zeal within the bounds of loving kindness to is to accept other people's hesitation to agree, or outright disagreement, graciously and gener-

---

5. Some Christians may find this discussion of religious zeal less than satisfactory because it subordinates "spreading the faith" to the ideal of loving kindness. This is an understandable concern, but it is well answered by Paul, who was anything but timid in his ministry. In 1 Corinthians 13, he wrote, "If I speak with the tongues of men and of angels, but do not have love, I have become a noisy gong or a clanging cymbal. . . . Love is patient, love is kind, and is not jealous; love does not brag and is not arrogant, does not act unbecomingly; it does not seek its own, is not provoked. . . . But now abide faith, hope, love, these three; but the greatest of these is love."

ously. Before you share any conviction with others, ask yourself what kind of reaction you expect from them. And be honest. Like many people, you may tell yourself you want only a fair hearing for your views when in reality you expect others to discard their convictions and embrace yours, totally and unconditionally. One good way to cut through any self-deception is to ask yourself if you've ever become upset and thought badly of others for not agreeing with you. Realizing that you have done so before can help you avoid doing so again.

After determining what you expect from people you want to persuade, ask yourself how you react when others try to persuade you. Do you feel comfortable having your views belittled and being badgered to accept theirs? Do you enjoy intimidation? If not, then be sure you refrain from these tactics yourself. On the other hand, if you enjoy feeling you can express reservations about the other person's views or reject them outright without incurring his or her displeasure, do your best to create that feeling in others.

Chapter 7

Habits that Foster Loving Kindness

Although habit is one of the most powerful factors in human behavior—someone once called it a "second nature"—self-improvement books seldom devote much attention to it. As a result, relatively few people have learned how to use it to their advantage.

Think of habit as a behavioral groove. Any response to a situation, if repeated a few times, develops such a groove. Whenever a similar situation arises and we react in the same way, the groove gets a little deeper. As time goes on, greater and greater effort is required to respond differently. Worse, the longer we remain in the groove, the more we *want* to remain in it. "This is the response that expresses my individuality, my uniqueness," we tell ourselves, forgetting that it began in a single act that we may have made impulsively, without even giving thought to the consequences.

Fortunately, any bad habit can be replaced with a good one. All that is required is to identify the good habit and then practice it long enough to form a new "groove." This approach can be used with any area of your life that you wish to improve; for example, you might want to become a better communicator or a more efficient worker. Our discussion will focus on the habits associated with loving kindness. Some of them have been mentioned briefly in previous chapters; others are new.

Count Your Blessings

Tina was an only child whose parents had doted on her from infancy and had treated her as an equal from early childhood, going so far as to consult her on the family menus and choice of furniture. They were also gifted professionals who loved learning and instilled that love in Tina. They even took her with them on their assignments around the globe so that she could gain first-hand understanding of a variety of peoples and cultures. Despite all this, when Tina was fifteen she became angry and rebellious, accusing her parents of denying her attention and freedom of choice.

The situation became more and more tense until Tina's grandfather took her aside for a frank discussion. He challenged her to compare her life with the lives of teenagers around the world and see whether her self-pity was justified. Accepting the challenge, Tina considered the deplorable conditions in which millions of young people, including some in her own country, have to live. She then considered her family's above average income, her upscale home and neighborhood, private school, wardrobe, health and dental care. Also, the many trips she had taken abroad and the relationships she had formed with people of diverse cultures. Most important of all, she remembered the myriad ways her parents had tried to make her happy.

By the time she finished this comparison, Tina understood that she was more privileged than the vast majority of young people *who ever lived.* By then her self-pity had dissolved and in its place was what Roman orator Cicero long ago termed "not only the greatest of virtues but the mother of all the rest"—a sense of gratitude.

Although Nathan's situation was in many respects different from Tina's, he learned the value of counting his blessings in a similar way. By the time he graduated from college, he was filled with resentment toward his parents. He remembered numerous occasions when their personalities clashed and caused tension for him and his siblings. He recalled vividly (and perhaps magnified) every harsh word they had spoken to him and every slight they had committed. Determined to get as far away from them and their midwestern American existence as possible, he moved to Malaysia.

After Nathan had been in Malaysia for a little over a year, something strange began to happen. He started to remember, one by one, his parents' acts of loving kindness toward their children. The hours they spent teaching them how to play various sports, especially tennis; the innumerable trips they took to tournaments around the state and beyond; the encouragement and (when necessary) consolation they offered. Those positive memories then triggered others—their efforts to make holidays special, their concern about schoolwork, the standard of integrity and responsibility they set for him and his siblings. Suddenly, Nathan's bad memories seemed so small and petty that he felt ashamed of himself for harboring them. He, too, felt grateful to his parents.

The fact that counting our blessings produces a sense of gratitude and motivates us to think, speak, act with loving kindness toward our benefactors makes it an excellent habit to develop. The first step in doing so is to take inventory of your blessings either mentally or, even better, in writing. General blessings include the gift of life and the means to sustain it—food, water, shelter, and clean air. Add the beauty of the earth and its breathtaking variety of plants, animals, and geography. More particular blessings include tools and utensils from frying pans and electricity to your car and computer. Don't forget important places that provide you services—hospitals, libraries, grocery stores, firehouses, police departments, and post offices. Most important, list the relationships that have enriched your life in great and small ways, past as well as present. (There is no statute of limitations on gratitude.) Keep this list in the forefront of your mind or in a prominent place in your home.

Next, reinforce your habit by making it your standard reaction in everyday situations. For example, when someone takes advantage of you, be grateful you are the victim and not the victimizer. When you become frustrated about a work assignment, be glad you have a job. When the traffic is moving too slowly for you, be happy you have someplace to go and a vehicle to take you there. When you can't afford a luxury item, remind yourself that millions of people can't afford the necessities of life. When the magazine or book you are reading seems dull, remember that an estimated one billion people have never learned to read and many more have no access to books or magazines. This focus on gratitude will make you will feel better and be kinder to others.

Cultivate Positive Emotions

Almost twenty-five hundred years ago, the Chinese philosopher Mencius explained the benefits of positive emotions. He wrote, "The feeling of compassion is the beginning of benevolence; the feeling of shame and self-reproach, the beginning of righteousness; the feeling of courtesy and modesty, the beginning of propriety; the feeling of right and wrong, the beginning of wisdom. These four beginnings are like the four limbs of man and to deny oneself any of these potentialities is to cripple oneself."

One of these emotions—shame—needs clarification. Mencius was not recommending a general, persistent feeling of shame, which would be unhealthy, but only the particular feeling that follows doing something wrong. In such situations, shame helps us take responsibility for our wrongdoing, make amends, and resolve to do better in the future.[1]

Mencius' list can be expanded, of course. One good addition is joy at other people's achievements. Another is appreciation of beauty and truth. Yet another is empathy, the ability to feel other people's disappointments and sufferings. All these emotions, especially the last, are associated with the practice of loving kindness.

Develop a Cheerful Demeanor

My wife and I recently shared an elevator with an elderly woman. The day was beautiful, sunny and warm with low humidity. My wife smiled at the woman and said, "Lovely day, isn't it?" The woman furrowed her brow and replied, "It'll be hot and muggy before long,

---

1. Some modern psychologists have argued that *all* feelings of shame are unhealthy. Unfortunately, such thinking implies that no behavior is ever unjustified. People who embrace this view risk the loss of conscience.

though, and I hate that weather." She was obviously the kind of person who brightens a room, or an elevator, by leaving it.

What does it take to be a room *brightening* person? What C. S. Lewis once described as "the unobtrusive talent for making all things at all times as cheerful and comfortable as circumstances [allow]." The essence of a cheerful demeanor is a pleasant outlook. This has been variously described as seeing the glass half-full rather than half-empty, choosing to walk on the sunny side of the street, and looking for the silver lining in the clouds of life.

You don't have to deny the existence of difficulties and problems to have a cheerful demeanor. Just show your faith that most difficulties aren't as bad as they seem and that every problem has a solution. One way to do this is to smile more. Another is to keep your complaints about people, things, and life to yourself unless you are sure that speaking will improve the situation; in other words, make it your rule never to utter a *gratuitously* harsh word. A third is to modulate your voice, eliminating any offensive qualities, such as shrillness or stridency, so that you sound as pleasant as you look.

Look for the Good in Others

Albert Einstein was curious about pictures he had seen of Mahatma Gandhi greeting others by bowing with his hands folded, as if in prayer. So he wrote and asked Gandhi to explain the greeting. Gandhi replied that it was summed up in the word *namastae*, which means "I honor the place in you where the entire universe resides. I honor the place in you of light, love, truth, peace, and wisdom. I honor the place in you where, when you are in that place, and I am in that place, there's only one of us."

This perspective may seem uniquely Hindu. Yet in a sense it is universal. Most religions believe there is goodness in people—a typical formulation is that people are "created in the image and likeness of God." The more we look for that goodness and focus on it, rather than on people's faults and flaws, the more inclined we will be to practice loving kindness.[2]

Looking for goodness in others is most difficult when their beliefs differ sharply from ours. The reason is that the differences keep distracting us. For example, a Presbyterian looking for goodness in Mormons may find her thoughts returning to the question of whether the Book of Mormon is compatible with the Bible. A Catholic looking for goodness in Jews may be diverted by the recurring thought that Jews do not accept Jesus as the Messiah. A Seventh Day Adventist looking for goodness in Muslims (or even other Christians) may be hampered by the thought that they keep holy the "wrong" Sabbath.

The solution is to focus on *the people themselves* rather than their theology.[3] That will permit you to see and admire, for example, the wonderful sense of community evident among Mormons, the impressive commitment of Jews to philanthropy, and Muslims' great devotion to prayer.

When you see goodness in an individual or group, religious or otherwise, that image will take root in your mind

---

2. The fact that in some people the goodness is buried rather deep is no excuse for not looking.

3. In doing this, you will not be saying that theology is unimportant or that all answers to important questions about God are equal. You will simply be suspending—for the moment—whatever is not relevant to your search.

and heart and make it easier for you to treat them with loving kindness. This is even true in the formal, supervisory relationships that occur in business. Barbara, a retired secretary, tells of her experiences with two bosses in a major corporation. One focused exclusively on the negative aspects of employee performance, apparently on the mistaken theory that compliments cause complacency. The other did not hesitate to criticize employees when necessary, but his emphasis was always on their good qualities. Not surprisingly, employees appreciated his kindness and performed much better for him than for the first boss.

Reflect Before Reacting

Impulsiveness often causes us to say and do things we later regret. Reflection enables us, instead, to evaluate our impressions and impulses and choose the most appropriate response. That is why the habit of reflection is a powerful aid to loving kindness. Reflection consists of three simple steps: suspending the impulse, asking pertinent questions, and finding the most reasonable answers.

Suppose you are driving in the center lane of the highway and someone races up on your right, passes you, then cuts across your lane and into the lane on the left. You immediately feel the urge to race after him, catch him at the next traffic light, and shout your disapproval of his driving. The reflective response would be to suspend the impulse and answer these questions: "Was that driver's behavior irresponsible and dangerous?" "Was I startled by it?" "Was I hurt?" "Will 'getting even' do any good?" "Could it conceivably do harm to myself and other drivers?" The answers—yes, yes, no, no, yes—will suggest a more sensible response, continuing at your pace and being grateful that no harm was done. (A modest epithet is permissible in such cases, if whispered to yourself.)

Now imagine that you have just heard someone say something you have grown tired of hearing. If you are white, the statement might express a black group's objection to "racial profiling." Or, if you are a gentile, it might express a Jewish recollection of the Holocaust. Your impulse may be to think "Always the same theme—will it never end!" and feel disgusted. The reflective response would be to stop and ask yourself, "How would I feel if the police stopped me for no other reason than the color of my skin?" or "How soon would I forget the extermination of millions of my people, including close relatives?" Your answer would likely make you feel more understanding and tolerant.

Similarly, if you are about to deny your child's request for time or attention, pause and ask yourself whether what you are doing is really so important. And if you are feeling offended over some slight by a friend or co-worker, ask if it might have been unintentional or whether it was too minor for you to warrant your concern.

Focus on the Present Moment

The Buddha advised his followers, "As you walk and eat and travel, be where you are. Otherwise you will miss most of your life." More recently, someone expressed the same thought a little more poetically: "Yesterday is history/Tomorrow is a mystery/Today is a gift/That's why it's called the present."

The present moment is the only time in which you can exercise your freedom to think, speak, and act. The past is a storehouse of experience, full of lessons and insight, a profitable place to visit but not to dwell in because everything there is dead and immutable. The future is a fascinating but elusive projection of hopes, dreams, and possibilities—always ahead of you, tantalizing but unapproachable.[4] Only the present moment, the point where C. S. Lewis said "time touches eternity," offers you opportunities to act and achieve. And the most precious of all are the opportunities to practice loving kindness.[5]

Unfortunately, when the opportunities are modest, the present moment can seem unexciting, and you may either lapse into the past—reliving joyous moments or lamenting shameful ones and wondering how your life would have been affected if you had made different choices—or daydream about the future. You may also persuade yourself that whatever small opportunities for loving kindness you miss by slipping out of the present moment can be made up for by seizing the grand opportunities. However, as Samuel Johnson observed, "he who waits to do a great deal of good at once will never do anything [because] life is made up of little things [and] true greatness consists in being great in little things." Mother Teresa of Calcutta was even more emphatic, claiming that "we can do no great things; only small things with great love."

Some of those "small things" often have a greater significance than we realize at the time. Nora, a young working woman in Chicago, was getting settled into her

---

4. The future is also the repository of good intentions, including the ones with which the road to hell is said to be paved.

5. Chiara Lubich's *Here and Now: Meditations on Living in the Present* (Hyde Park: New City Press, 2000) is an excellent source of insight on the concept of the present moment.

new apartment when her mother called and asked if she would mind driving her and Nora's father for a visit to their former home, several hours away. (Her father, having recently had a heart attack, could not drive and her mother felt uncomfortable doing so.) Nora was tempted to say she was too busy to go, but she decided to make the sacrifice in the name of love. In years to come she would be grateful for having seized that little opportunity, for during that trip her father suffered a massive stroke and died in her arms.

Take the Initiative in Loving

Some people sincerely want to practice loving kindness, and remain alert for opportunities to do so. But then, when an opportunity arises, they become timid. They think "I'm not sure how the person will respond, so I'd better play it safe and say (or do) nothing." A classic case concerns people's avoidance of funerals because they "don't know what to say" to the grieving family. In reality, it is not necessary to say anything. Simply being there conveys the appropriate sentiment. And a clasp of the hand, an arm around the shoulder, or a friendly embrace can be as comforting as the most eloquent words.

Other people are timid in situations where they can't be sure of what reaction their gesture will produce. So they wait for the other person to take the initiative. In many cases, that never happens, and the opportunity is lost.

The Baal Shem Tov, who founded the Hasidic movement, offers a simple yet effective suggestion for overcoming such timidity: "When you meet somebody, you should say to yourself, 'I'm going to fulfill the command-

ment to love my neighbor, with this person before me.'"
In short, don't speculate or agonize over whether to take
the initiative. Just take it. You'll almost always be glad
that you did.

When Tanya, a saleswoman, walked into a customer's
waiting room, she noticed a former customer of hers who
was now a competitor. Because she felt awkward, her first
thought was to wait and let the other woman speak first.
Then she decided to take the initiative. She greeted the
woman, congratulated her on her new job, and wished her
well. The woman seemed surprised but was noticeably
pleased at Tanya's graciousness.

Barry faced a much more difficult challenge. He
worked as a counselor and weight-lifting coach at a rehabilitation center for juvenile offenders, ages fourteen to
eighteen, who had been convicted of such crimes as rape,
arson, burglary, and robbery. On Barry's second day on
the job, one of the inmates bit a counselor, kicked another
young man in the mouth, and cursed at and threatened
the other counselors. In order to restrain him, Barry had
to sit on him. Though such serious incidents happened
only about once a month, the potential for them was
constant, and Barry quickly learned to rely on force to
maintain order.

Then one day Barry reflected on the irony that the
counselors were using force to teach the inmates not to
use force. He began to think that loving kindness might
be a more sensible approach, but he feared that trying it
would make the other counselors think he was crazy.
Eventually, however, he got the courage to do so. The first
test came when he tried to stop a fight between inmates
and was himself hit in the mouth. He managed to stifle his
anger and not to retaliate. Next he sought ways of prac-

ticing loving kindness. He began helping inmates with their chores, such as cleaning toilets and vacuuming, and went out of his way to be cooperative to other staff members. Soon the other staff members began to imitate Barry's approach. One used his own money to buy art supplies for the inmates. Others gave them clothing. Before long, the inmates began to show to one another the respect and concern the counselors were modeling.

Disagree Without Being Disagreeable

Wherever two or more people are engaged in discussion, there is likely to be a disagreement, and the more serious and significant the topic, the greater the likelihood. It is possible to disagree without being disagreeable, but the horrible example of many radio and television talk shows has obscured this fact. All too often, rudeness is confused with intellectual rigor. A typical pattern is for the host to ask a question, the guest to begin responding, the host to say "You're not answering the question," the guest to beg "Let me answer," and the host to ignore the plea and proceed to answer his own question. When two guests are present, the situation is often worse. One guest begins to speak, the other interrupts, the first one objects, the host calls for order, then everyone abandons decorum and talks at the same time. At the end of the program, the host thanks the guests for their "vigorous and insightful debate."

Anyone who watches such pathetic excuses for debate may unconsciously imitate the behavior he or she sees there. If you are such a person, you can restore civility to your discussions by adopting two simple rules. The first is to let minor differences in discussion pass without comment. Doing this in no way compromises your integrity but is simply a mark of forbearance.

The second rule concerns more significant differences of opinion. When they occur, resist the urge to browbeat the other person into agreeing with you. That urge may seem to reflect commitment to your beliefs; often as not, however, it reflects a prideful "mine is better" attitude, an unrealistic expectation, or both. Focus on presenting your view to the best of your ability and listen politely and attentively to the other person's view. If he raises questions about any of your points, answer calmly and patiently. If you ask him questions, allow him to answer without interruption.

According to an ancient Chinese saying, the first one to raise his or her voice in a discussion thereby admits defeat. By applying this saying and remaining polite and respectful of others even in the heat of vigorous debate, you will provide a model of loving kindness.

Treat Everyone as Your Superior

Even in a democracy it is common to show special courtesy to wealthy people, holders of important positions in government or industry, and celebrities. The same behavior occurs in the workplace. Teachers are deferential to the principal, nurses to doctors, and bank or factory employees to supervisors and executive officers. In the case of celebrities, the reason for the special treatment is adulation; in the other cases, prudence. Rudeness to those who have power over you could lead to unemployment. Yours!

On the other hand, if you are like most people, you are less vigilant about how you treat your equals and subordinates—the people who work with or for you, your family, friends, and neighbors. They pose little immediate threat to your security and you feel no adulation toward them (though in some cases you should), so you don't feel the same need to treat them well.

An excellent way to improve your practice of loving kindness is to form the habit of treating everyone you encounter as if he or she were an important person. Though this may seem an odd way to behave, it is really quite reasonable because, given that everyone possesses human dignity, everyone *really is* an important person.

I recently used this approach with one of the most difficult types of people to be nice to, a telephone solicitor. I prepared in advance by reminding myself that people who do this work are trying, like the rest of us, to earn a living and support their families; that they experience more rejection in an hour than most people encounter in a couple of weeks; and that it wouldn't take me any longer to be kind than to be cruel. Then I filed these thoughts away and waited.

My opportunity came, appropriately enough, while working on an earlier chapter of this book. The phone rang, I answered, and a young woman said, "Hi, I'm Rainbow and I'd like to talk to you about insurance today." I quickly asked myself how I could treat her as an important person. The answer came instantly—I could show interest in her name. So I said, "Excuse me for interrupting, Rainbow. I have all the health insurance I need. But how did you get your lovely name?" I could almost hear her smile as she said enthusiastically, "My parents wanted to choose an unusual name." I then said they chose well and thanked her for calling.

Be Sparing with Advice

Nothing can seem as unkind as unwanted advice. It doesn't matter how well-intentioned or, for that matter, how insightful the advice may be. In fact, the more insightful it is, the more people may resent it, even if they asked for it. This odd dynamic—being offended for getting what one has requested—is easily explained. When people ask for our "honest opinion," they do not necessarily want it but may merely be seeking agreement with a conclusion they have already reached but haven't bothered to express.

For example, "How does this jacket look on me?" could be shorthand for "I have decided to buy this jacket and I want you to endorse my decision." If that is the case, "I think it is the wrong color for you" will not be well received. Sometimes the situation is even more complex. If a friend recounts an argument she had with her husband and asks whether her view was right, you could be in trouble no matter how you answer. If you say "no," her feelings may be hurt; if you say "yes" and she tells her husband, his feelings may be hurt. Quite possibly, by the time they finish their discussion, both will agree you should have minded your own business.

Of course, negative consequences are surer and often more serious when your advice is unsolicited. In light of all these considerations, the ideal of loving kindness is best served if you give advice sparingly. If it is not asked for, don't volunteer it.[6] If it is asked for, be honest but

---

6. The only exception is a situation in which the person's health or safety is at risk and the person has not received the advice before. (Note: nagging about smoking or excess weight doesn't qualify here.)

gentle and say no more than is necessary. However, if you suspect the person wants approval rather than candid assessment, consider saying , "Have you already made up your mind? If so, I'd prefer not to take a chance on upsetting you."

Forgive Others' Offenses

Although we discussed forgiveness at some length in chapter 1, two additional points should be made. The first concerns how many times you should forgive a person before saying "Enough!" This is the very question Peter the Apostle asked Jesus. Peter thought that up to seven times would be reasonable. Jesus replied, "Not up to seven times, but up to seventy times seven." It would be difficult to keep count that long, of course, and that was precisely the point Jesus was making—a truly forgiving person doesn't keep score.

The second point concerns whether you should withhold forgiveness until the offender apologizes or otherwise shows contrition. A little reflection on your personal experience of *committing* offenses will suggest an answer to that question. Do you apologize for your offenses immediately after you commit them? Do you, instead, wait until the offended person complains to you? Do you wait even longer than that—days, weeks, or even months?

Do you ever avoid apologizing at all and just hope that the offended person will forget? In fairness you should expect others to be no quicker to apologize than you are.

The problem with withholding forgiveness for even a brief time is that we hurt ourselves as much as, if not more than, the other person. Resentment undermines our emotional health and makes it difficult for us to practice loving kindness. Thus the sooner we forgive others, the better—for us as well as the other person.

Apologize When You Offend

Simple fairness demands that we be as ready to accept blame as we are to assign it to others. We are not, of course, as is evident from the way we typically describe events. If someone else gets angry with us, we say "he got angry." However, if we get angry with him, we say "he made me angry." If someone is late for an appointment with us, we say "she kept me waiting"; but if we are late, we say "I couldn't get there on time." In other words, we tend to hold others responsible not only for their own offenses but for ours as well. And if we can't blame others (it would be absurd to blame the person we kept waiting for causing our tardiness), we blame circumstances or fate.

Similarly, we say "That's the way I am" to excuse something we did. But if someone who offended us uses that expression, we quickly point out that such an excuse is unacceptable. Also, we seldom hesitate to suggest that other people deserved our ill treatment but somehow are never willing to admit that we deserved theirs.

These face-saving maneuvers come so naturally to most of us that it takes continuing effort to resist them and take responsibility for our offenses. To appreciate the value of that effort, you need only think of a time when someone offered you a sincere apology for a word or action that injured you and recall how much better that apology made you feel about the other person, yourself, and your relationship. You can give others that same feeling, and renew it in yourself, by apologizing for your offenses. The habit of doing this is an especially impressive indication of loving kindness.

Associate with Loving People

Research has shown that when our environment changes, our attitudes and values are altered, sometimes profoundly. A young person who joins a gang, for example, will begin dressing, talking, acting, and perhaps even thinking differently. So will someone who leaves a small town and attends a large university, or who joins a religious order, moves to a foreign country, or spends time in prison. Knowing this, wise people ask themselves from time to time whether the individuals they are associating with and the groups they belong to are helping them be the kind of people they aspire to be.

If you wish to become more proficient in practicing loving kindness, you should consider joining a group dedicated to that ideal. For example, if there is a chapter of Habitat for Humanity near you, you can volunteer to build homes for the poor. Or you can work in a shelter for the homeless or a literacy program, or become a Big Brother or Big Sister to a child that needs mentoring.

There are also many religious organizations dedicated to loving kindness. For example, Operation Refuah is a global project that encourages Jews to practice the mitzvah of "Love your neighbor as yourself." And the Hindu Swadhyaya movement is based on the "twin pillars of selfless love and selfless work." It aims to spread the message that everyone, whether rich or poor, possesses an "inner divinity" and therefore should be treated with respect and love. Your church or temple may be able to provide information about other organizations of this kind.

There are also groups that aim to cultivate mutual love among people of all faiths, cultures, and racial/ethnic groups. One such group which has had a profound impact on my life is the Focolare Movement. In fact, my association with the movement inspired me to write this book.

Focolare is the Italian word for "hearth," a symbol of warmth, safety, and harmony. The movement began in 1943 in war-torn Italy, when a young woman named Chiara Lubich and her young women friends saw their city of Trent devastated and their lives disrupted. They wondered, "Is anything in this life permanent?" and their answer, "Only God," prompted them to read the Bible during the many hours they spent in air raid shelters. They were especially drawn to the numerous passages on love, notably Jesus' direction to "love one another as I have loved you," and his prayer "that all may be one."

These passages gave the young women's lives a new foundation and purpose. They would strive to achieve unity of spirit with everyone they encountered, seize every opportunity for a specific act of love, and take the initiative in loving without pausing to wonder whether the other person was appreciative. In these efforts the Gospel was their guide. Each week they would take a specific passage—they called it a "word of life"—and seek ways to apply it. Later they would recount their experiences to one another. This sharing, combined with the practice of treating one another as they would treat Jesus, nurtured their mutual love.

Today the Focolare Movement has more than six million members and friends in 180 countries; twenty "model towns"; and numerous publishing houses, magazines, and newsletters. Each month Chiara Lubich's reflection on the "Word of Life" is published in ninety languages and dialects and is read or heard by an estimated fourteen million people.

A key reason for the Focolare Movement's wide appeal is its unique perspective on the goal of spiritual unity. Historically, doctrinal agreement was believed to be the necessary foundation for such unity. Given the bewildering variety of specific beliefs, such agreement seems unlikely at best. Some people say God exists, others say there is no God, still others await scientific proof that is not available now and perhaps will never be. Polytheists assert that there are many deities, monotheists say there is but one. Among the latter, there is further disagreement over the divine nature, with Christians claiming three persons—Father, Son, and Holy Spirit—in one divine nature; and Muslims and Jews affirming a single person and nature. Similar division exists within the various religions over innumerable component beliefs. For these reasons, however much people of faith may yearn for unity, most believe there is nothing they can do to bring it about except to pray that professional theologians will discover a resolution to doctrinal differences.

The Focolare perspective on unity is very different and much more hopeful. It holds that, though theological agreement is desirable, it is not a precondition for spiritual unity. Further, that since unity concerns the heart as much as the mind, its challenge is not for trained theologians alone. Every individual has a contribution to make. Finally, that the foundation for unity does not need to be established because it *already exists* in the essential nature of every human being. As Chiara Lubich explains, "Brotherhood is in the DNA of every person created in the image and likeness of God." The secret of unity is to recognize that image and likeness in our neighbor and respond to it with loving kindness.

The Focolare understanding of unity explains why, though the movement is strongly rooted in Roman Catholic Christianity, its focus is not proselytizing but responding to the divine love that already exists in other people. When other Christians, Jews, Muslims, Buddhists, and Hindus become acquainted with the movement, they are inspired to a deeper appreciation of *their own* religious tradition's call to love. Meanwhile, agnostics and atheists feel not the usual pressure to abandon their viewpoint and give assent to alien dogma but instead a genuine spiritual kinship, a bond of love.

In January 2002 the Focolare was actively involved in the Vatican-sponsored day of prayer in Assisi, Italy. The participants included representatives of eighteen Orthodox churches, Roman Catholics, Anglicans, Presbyterians, Lutherans, Methodists, Baptists, members of the Salvation Army, Quakers, Disciples of Christ, Jews, Muslims, Buddhists, Tenrikyoists, Shintoists, Jainists, Sikhs, Hindus, Zoroastrians, and traditional African religionists.

Remain Vigilant

This habit is necessary because, being imperfect, we are all susceptible to backsliding. Suppose you decide that you are inordinately proud of yourself and your accomplishments and resolve to become more humble. After months of effort, you reach your goal, only to realize that you are now inordinately *proud of your humility!*

Old habits have a way of resurfacing long after we think we have overcome them. For example, a young Buddhist monk described an incident that occurred during a visit to his native Australia after three years in a Thai monastery. During his visit, he decided to spend a day meditating in a Buddhist center to maintain the serenity of mind he had acquired in the monastery. His father drove him to the center and picked him up later in the day. On the way home, in the course of conversation, his father mentioned some bad habits his son had had in adolescence and the young monk felt a "ball of fire flaring" in his belly. Despite his effort to control it, he succumbed and flew into a rage for which he was immediately ashamed.

We are most vulnerable to backsliding when we are relaxed, and we are most relaxed when with our friends and loved ones. That is why it is often more difficult to practice loving kindness with the people closest to us than with strangers. The solution is to be even more vigilant at such times. The following verse by Frank Outlaw summarizes both the how and the why of vigilance:

Watch your thoughts; they become words.
Watch your words; they become actions.
Watch your actions; they become habits.
Watch your habits; they become character.
Watch your character; it becomes your destiny.

Chapter 8

The Rewards of Loving Kindness

Sometime around 550 B.C., the Greek fablist Aesop wrote, "No act of kindness, no matter how small, is ever wasted." That encouraging assessment has reverberated down through the ages. In our time, however, a more cynical view has arisen: "No good deed goes unpunished." Admittedly, cases can be cited in support of the latter view. For example, when someone tries to bring warring spouses together and both turn against her. And when a whistleblower reports illegal actions in his company or government agency and is blackballed as a result. Far more often, however, Aesop's view proves to be the more insightful, particularly when we look beyond the immediate and obvious effects to more remote and subtle ones. In fact, small acts of loving kindness frequently produce disproportionately *larger* rewards, as the experience of Lola, a good friend of mine, illustrates.

Lola, a single professional woman in her early forties, was visiting her mother who lived in a retirement community in Florida. Each day Lola would spend some time sitting by the pool and reading. Each day she noticed an older woman swimming laps in the pool. Lola was struck with the effortless grace of her strokes. One day, after finishing her regimen, the swimmer introduced herself to

Lola and began talking. Unfortunately for Lola, the conversation was completely one-way. Later that day, she asked her mother about the woman and her mother explained that she was a retired concert pianist whom everyone in the community avoided because of her incessant talking.

The next day, as Lola again sat by the pool reading, she noticed the woman approaching and felt the urge to leave. But then she remembered the commitment she had made to treat everyone with love. " 'Everyone' includes this woman," she thought, and greeted the woman with a sincere compliment—"You swim so gracefully that it's a pleasure to watch you."

"Don't you swim?" the woman asked.

"Yes, but not well," Lola responded.

"Then get into the pool and I'll help you improve."

Lola spent much of the remainder of her visit in the pool mastering the various strokes and the proper way to breathe while swimming. The role of teacher exposed a very different side of the woman's personality. She listened as much as she talked, and Lola found her a wise and charming companion. The apparent change in the woman was not lost on the other members of the community. From the time of Lola's visit, her mother later informed her, the woman was no longer shunned.

The obvious and immediate rewards of Lola's loving kindness were increased proficiency in swimming and the pleasure of knowing that her benefactor was now accepted in the community. Grateful for both, she returned to her life in Chicago. One of the first things she did on arriving was to join a club so that she could take advantage of her new-found swimming skill on a regular basis. At the time she had no way of knowing that a much greater reward lay several years ahead, during another vacation with her mother.

Gene was still grieving the loss of his wife to cancer almost a year earlier. He had just sold his home in Virginia, packed up the few things he wanted to keep, and moved to Florida. When Gene and his grandson had finished unloading the contents of the trailer into Gene's new condominium, his grandson suggested they go for a swim in the pool. Gene consented, more out of kindness toward his grandson than out of any desire of his own. When they got to the pool, they found only one person swimming, someone who had been an ardent swimmer for several years and was taking advantage of the final hour of her vacation visit—Lola. As they exchanged pleasantries by the pool, Lola and Gene felt a mutual attraction which led to a long distance relationship and, eventually, to marriage. In the fifteen years she has been married to Gene, Lola has often reflected on how amply she has been rewarded for that one small act of kindness to a lonely woman. She is convinced of the accuracy of the promise that "God will not be outdone in generosity."

Some people are hesitant about making connections between events so far removed in time, of course. And they are even more inclined to balk when the intervening years are filled with suffering, as they were in the case of Viktor Frankl, the psychiatrist mentioned in chapter 1. Shortly before World War II, Frankl was offered a university position in the United States. At the time he was living in Vienna and was concerned about leaving his parents behind because the political situation was becoming dangerous for Jews. One day, as he was pondering whether to go to the United States or to stay in Vienna, he saw a piece of stone on his parents' dining room table. When he inquired about it, his father explained that he had picked it up in the rubble of a synagogue that had been destroyed by the Nazis. The stone was part of the tables of the Ten Commandments, and the letter on the stone was an abbreviation of one of the Commandments, "Honor thy father and thy mother." Frankl regarded this not as a coincidence but as an answer to his question. Accordingly, he declined the invitation to leave the country.

Frankl's original fears proved prophetic. His whole family was sent to, and eventually perished in, the concentration camps. Moreover, Frankl himself spent time in four camps, and when he was first incarcerated, a manuscript he considered his most significant scholarly achievement was taken from him and destroyed. Certainly, none of this could reasonably be classified as a reward, divine or otherwise, for his act of loving kindness to his parents. In fact, it seems more like the kind of punishment cynics associate with good deeds. But there is more to the story.

The concentration camp experience gave Frankl the opportunity to test, through his own experiences and those of other inmates, the reigning psychological views of human nature. Sigmund Freud had maintained that the main drive in human beings is the sex drive; Adler claimed it was the drive for power. Their theories were largely speculative, drawn as they were from generally abnormal patients' personal histories, and untested in anything resembling a laboratory setting. In contrast, Frankl was not only able to observe tens of thousands of normal people suffering extreme deprivation in a controlled situation, but also to suffer the same deprivation with them. He found that long after the drive for sex and/or power had flickered and died, the drive to find meaning in one's life remained.

After the war, Frankl wrote many profound works, among them the moving—indeed, inspiring—account of his observations in the camps, *Man's Search for Meaning*. He also developed a unique system of psychotherapy based on the human drive for meaning and continued to contribute insights to the field of psychiatry for a half-century after the war. Perhaps he would have been an excellent psychiatrist had he gone to the United States instead of staying with his parents in Vienna. But he would surely not have made the particular contributions for which he is remembered. Those contributions were a result of his act of loving kindness for his parents.

What Rewards Can You Expect

There is no magic formula for determining the specific rewards the practice of loving kindness will produce for you. They are likely to vary in kind and intensity. Some will be so modest as to be unremarkable; others will be significant. Many will change your life, but more often than not this will happen so incrementally that you may hardly notice any difference in yourself. Nevertheless, it is possible to identify six broad areas in which you can expect to be rewarded.

Loving kindness will deepen your humanity

This means simply that loving kindness will enable you to display more of the good qualities and fewer of the bad qualities associated with being human. It is a truism that our thoughts, words, and actions shape our identity.

Remember the story of the woman whose dog bit a newspaper boy. When he reported the incident to the authorities, the woman began a vendetta against him that
continued unabated for *forty-five years*. For all those years
she freely chose to be a vengeful, mean-spirited person. As
we noted, she could as easily have chosen to respond to
the newspaper boy with loving kindness. And what a
difference it would have made in her life!

Compare her response with that of Etty Hillesum, a pris-
oner in the Nazi concentration camp at Auschwitz. While
being victimized by genuine evil, Hillesum chose to practice
love. The diaries she left behind expressed the intensity of
her motivation. She wrote, "I love people so [deeply],
because in every human being I love something of You
[God]. And I seek You everywhere in them." Also, "Against
every new outrage and every fresh horror we shall put up
one more piece of love and goodness" and "We should be
willing to act as balm for all wounds." Consider, too, the
example of the Tibetan monk who, when the Chinese
invaders took over his monastery, set himself a single
goal—to maintain loving kindness toward the Chinese
people no matter how badly their soldiers treated him.

Hillesum and the monk undoubtedly had the same
ignoble urges as the rest of us and very likely faced the
same temptation to give in to those urges and remain less
than they were capable of being. What made them
different—that is, more fully human—is that they chose
to resist those urges and instead practice loving kindness.

Loving kindness will make you happier and healthier

Many of the stories of loving kindness throughout this
book have underscored the relationship between loving
kindness and happiness. A good example is the story of

Casey, who gave his expensive football jersey to an injured teenager. Not only did the gift have the expected effect with the teenager; it also brought unexpected joy to Casey. He later commented that the gratification he experienced from giving away the jersey far outweighed its monetary and sentimental value, for in doing so he felt "God's pleasure."

Another example is the story of Brad, the teenager who decided to regard his chores as opportunities to express gratitude rather than as a burden to be resented. He then began to work more diligently and each day tried to do something extra. When his mother noticed the change in him and started complimenting him, a sense of pride and satisfaction replaced his feeling of resentment. Before long, he no longer dreaded his chores but actually looked forward to them.

One of the most moving and meaningful of all the stories we have discussed is the story of Anthony, the young Italian immigrant who never forgot the kindness of the stranger who gave him the four dollars that enabled him to remain in the United States. Unable to find the man, he decided to repay his kindness in the only way he could—by passing it on to anyone he found in need. That decision not only kept his gratitude alive; it also ensured that he would always be a happy man.

In addition to making you happier, loving kindness will also make you healthier. Medical research has revealed that a great deal of physical illness can be traced to the anxiety that accompanies suspicion, resentment, and anger. Loving kindness displaces those "afflictive emotions" and replaces them with trust, compassion, and amity. As a result, you will be less susceptible to diseases of mind and body.

Everyday experience confirms this finding. If you are like most people, an unpleasant encounter leaves you feeling upset, and angry thoughts at bedtime disturb your sleep. Conversely, pleasant encounters are calming and loving thoughts promote restful sleep. Surely Bernard Baruch had these facts in mind when he said, as we noted earlier, "One of the secrets of a long and fruitful life is to forgive everybody everything every night before you go to bed."

Loving kindness will bring out the best in others

Arlene was visiting a relative in a nursing home. As she walked down the hall, she passed a male resident who shouted in a nasty voice, "Why are you looking at me like that?" Arlene's first impulse was to respond, "What are you talking about, you old coot. No one is looking at you." But she stifled that reaction and said, matter-of-factly, "That's a nice shirt you have on and it looks good on you." The man gave her a wide smile in reply.

Marian's seven-year-old son Charles hated his school reading assignments and did his best to neglect them. Marian tried yelling, badgering, cajoling, and threatening, but nothing worked. Then, in desperation, she decided on a more loving approach—giving up her time and sitting with him as he read. At first, when she had him read aloud, he tried his best to upset her. For example, he would speed up or slow down, deliberately mispronounce words, or twist and twitch as if he had the condition once known as "St. Vitus' dance." But through it all, Marian remained calm. Then, quite abruptly, Charles began reading properly. And a few sessions later he said to her, "Mom, you don't have to sit with me any more. I'll read my assignments on my own."

Remember Piyapañño, the Buddhist monk from Australia, who found himself staring at the drunken deliveryman's fist poised a few inches from his face. Piyapañño stood silently, with his arms at his side, and concentrated on feeling loving kindness toward the aggressor. After a moment, the deliveryman's anger dissolved. No doubt you have had similar, if less potentially violent, experiences. For example, a situation in which you apologized for having quarreled with someone and had the other person say, "I'm sorry for my part in the quarrel, too."

The principle underlying all these examples is *like begets like*. When you take the initiative in expressing loving kindness, you encourage others to respond in kind. The response may not be immediate; some people are adept at resisting their gentler impulses, often for years. But given enough time and good example, most will succumb.

We have been focusing on the responses of people to whom loving kindness is directly expressed, yet it can also bring out the best in people who merely see or hear of it. Human beings are imitative creatures: they tend to follow what is fashionable, not just in clothing and hairstyles, but also in the treatment of others. Fashions, of course, do not spring from the void—they come about when one or more individuals diverge from the crowd. That is how the current plague of rudeness and incivility began. It is also how it will end. Your example of loving kindness can hasten that happy event.

Loving kindness will fight prejudice

The Golden Rule specifies that we are to treat others as we would have others treat us. No normal person would want to be denied his or her individuality and lumped in with tens of thousands or millions of other people whose only similarity is skin color, cultural heritage, language, or religious tradition. No one would want to be regarded as possessing undesirable traits, particularly traits formulated in bigots' overactive imaginations, and never given a chance to prove otherwise. Yet this is just what prejudice does to people.

Because prejudice is inherently unkind, loving kindness is its natural antidote. By practicing loving kindness in your dealings with others, particularly those who have been victimized by prejudice and discrimination, you will help to banish stereotypes, dissolve suspicion and distrust, and build mutual respect and good will.

Loving kindness will help solve social problems

In earlier chapters, we noted a number of examples of how loving kindness helped to solve social problems. One was Karen Graham's founding of the William S. Graham Foundation for Melanoma Research to raise public awareness and fund research initiatives in the fight against the disease that claimed her son. Another was Cindi Lamb's and Candace Lightner's creation of Mothers Against Drunk Driving (MADD). Also, Millard Fuller's Habitat for Humanity, which builds homes for low income families, and Craig Kielburger's Free the Children, which he started when he was only twelve years old. Many other examples could be cited. Virtually every initiative to solve any social problem—from drug addiction to unemployment, child pornography, and the abuse of the elderly—begins in compassion for the victims.

When social problems remain unsolved, the reason generally involves a lack of loving kindness. This is particularly true in government, where narrow self-interest, blind party loyalty, and a spirit of divisiveness frequently block needed reforms in taxation, health care, and social security. Some say that to expect loving kindness to permeate bureaucracies is unrealistic. But it has happened, at least on a small scale, as the following story from Italy documents.

One official was disgusted with the disunity on the town council and resolved to overcome it. He began to practice loving kindness by increasing the involvement of opposition party members in important decisions, respecting their administrative mandates, and looking for the value in their proposals rather than opposing them for the sake of party loyalty. Soon the council atmosphere began to change. Dialogue replaced diatribe, personal relations were improved, and inter-party consultation increased. As a result, issues that had gone unresolved for years were settled, often by unanimous vote.

In addition to meeting the needs of the town, the council was able, with the approval of the citizens, to make small contributions to developing countries. For example, they helped finance the construction of a social welfare center in the Amazon and the rebuilding of a town in war-ravaged Bosnia.

Loving kindness will foster peace among nations

No one whose heart was filled with loving kindness ever lashed out with a fist, attacked another person with a knife or gun, or carried out a suicide bombing mission. Dictators and tyrants know this; that is why they foment suspicion and animosity among their followers. They realize that the moment people begin to regard their enemies as brothers and sisters and feel empathy for them, they will no longer be capable of hatred or violence.

Unfortunately, this hopeful truth is all too easily forgotten at a time when inhumanity dominates the news. That is why it is important to recall it and acknowledge the role loving kindness must play in the cause of peace among nations.

In 1993, after hate-inspired arsonists destroyed the house of a Turkish family in Solingen, Germany, a group of people held a peace conference and launched "Operation One for One" with the goal of establishing the bonds of friendship across ethnic lines. The effort was focused on four groups—Germans, Turks, Italians, and Koreans. The program was simple: Each individual was challenged to make a commitment to befriend at least one person of another nationality. That effort soon expanded and a network of "international cafes" was established. The term denotes monthly meetings at which people of different cultures share their customs, experiences, aspirations, and hopes. Those who attend believe that the bonds they are forming will provide a foundation for understanding among the various ethnic groups and, in time, make hate crimes nothing more than a bad memory.

Maria was employed as a secretary in a school in northern Spain, a stronghold of the Basque Separatist Movement (ETA). As a way of putting pressure on the government to acknowledge and respect Basque culture, the ETA pressured the school into forbidding access to anyone who did not speak the Basque language. Maria was expected to enforce the rule, but she regarded it as unfair, so she began admitting everyone without distinction. She knew that she might lose her job and perhaps even become a target of violence, but she decided that her acts of loving kindness were more important than her comfort or safety. Eventually, her superiors discovered the violation but, amazingly, they ignored it. In fact, word got to Maria that they secretly approved of her actions.

Emboldened by her success in showing loving kindness in the school, Maria joined her friends in public protests against terrorist violence in her region. On one day of every week at 8:00 a.m., in more than a hundred locations, Maria and others gathered in their neighborhoods and public squares and spent fifteen minutes in peaceful, prayerful silence. Doing this took courage because extremists also attended the gatherings to threaten, intimidate, and harass the demonstrators. What made these occasions especially chilling was the fact that some of the antagonists were the demonstrators' colleagues and neighbors. Nevertheless, the protests changed some minds and instilled a sense of hope. As a man said to the demonstrators, "Today I have discovered that there is a new generation and a new hope, for the future has been born in my heart."

In 1991, Paul and Rachel and their two children moved from their native Albania to Israel. The adjustment was not too difficult because, though Paul is Christian, Rachel is Jewish. Nevertheless, they immediately felt the tension between the Jews and the Arabs. It existed almost everywhere except in the meetings of the Focolare Movement that, because of its emphasis on mutual love and unity, welcomes all people. In those meetings the spirit of brotherhood remained strong, even when Israeli/Palestinian clashes were at their worst. For example, in early 2002, after the terrorist attacks on Tel Aviv and Jerusalem, Paul and Rachel organized a two-day Focolare meeting in a nearby village. Although travel on the roads was dangerous, many Jews, Christians, and Muslims attended.

The degree of progress these examples represent is so small, and the ultimate reward for them is so remote that you may be inclined to dismiss them as inconsequential. Yet as an ancient Chinese proverb wisely notes, "A journey of a thousand miles begins with a single step." Every step in such a journey is valuable because it brings us closer to the destination. The same relationship exists between each act of loving kindness and the goal of world peace.

Afterword

As we noted in the Preface, the legacy of September 11, 2001 is part inspiration and part perplexity. The inspiration came from witnessing countless acts of loving kindness, even to the point of people giving their lives for their neighbors. What we saw reminded us of a moral ideal more sensible and satisfying than the reigning selfism and relativism. Many of us also experienced anew certain emotions now considered antiquated—affection for our country and respect for its principles, disappointment that we have not always lived up to our highest ideals, and a desire to emulate the heroes among us.

The perplexity lay in the difficult questions prompted by the loving kindness evident after September 11: Why does it take a tragedy to produce such an outpouring of loving kindness? How can that kindness be cultivated in more normal circumstances? What can be done to prevent self-absorption from blinding us to others' needs? How can our desire to love be translated into concrete action and directed not just to those we admire or pity but to all people?

The answer to the first question is that we humans are an imperfect species. We have the potential to be caring or uncaring, selfless or selfish, loving or hateful. Unfortunately, sustained effort is required to acquire and maintain the more positive qualities. Our situation is like that of a man walking up on a down escalator. The challenge facing him is achievable, but only if he keeps walking briskly. If he slows his pace, he quickly returns to his starting point.

We are most strongly tempted to relax our efforts toward moral excellence when life is going well. But when tragedies occur and we are confronted with vivid images of suffering, we feel compassion for the victims and are moved to expressions of loving kindness.

The other questions all concern how loving kindness can be cultivated in the absence of tragedy. The answer, as we have seen, has several dimensions. We must understand the various ways in which loving kindness can be expressed—in thought, word, deed, and silence—and draw encouragement from the good example of others. We must recognize the obstacles to loving kindness and the strategies that will enable us to surmount them. And we must develop the various habits that foster loving kindness and practice them faithfully so that we can resist the temptation to moral laxity.

When you have accomplished all this, only one challenge remains—to maintain your faith in the value of your efforts. With ethnic hatreds, civil wars, and terrorist attacks constantly in the news and the most powerful nations in the world unable to find solutions, it is natural to wonder whether your small contributions of loving kindness can make a difference. Whenever you are in this frame of mind, remember the parable of the mustard seed, which is "smaller than all other seeds; but when it is fully grown, it is larger than the garden plants, and becomes a tree, so that the birds of the air come and nest in its branches." Each of our good deeds is such a seed.

And when the challenge of expressing loving kindness grows burdensome or your expressions of loving kindness are misunderstood or unappreciated and you entertain thoughts of giving up, turn to these encouraging words, which were recently posted on the internet without attribution:

People are often unreasonable, illogical, and self-centered; forgive them anyway.

If you are kind, people may accuse you of selfish, ulterior motives; be kind anyway.

If you are successful, you will win some false friends and some true enemies; succeed anyway.

If you are honest and frank, people may cheat you; be honest and frank anyway.

What you spend years building, someone could destroy overnight; build anyway.

If you find serenity and happiness, there may be jealousy; be happy anyway.

The good you do today, people will often forget tomorrow; do good anyway.

Give the world the best you have, and it may never be enough; give the world the best you've got anyway.

You see, in the final analysis, it is between you and God; it was never between you and them anyway.

Acknowledgments

The examples of loving kindness presented in this book have been drawn from the experiences of numerous individuals from a variety of cultures. My principal sources were *Living City Magazine,* which has for years invited readers to share their experiences of love of neighbor; fellow members of the Focolare Movement; and my friends and family.

Most of these accounts of loving kindness are not well known, in some cases not known at all, mainly because the people involved have had no desire for recognition. To preserve their privacy, I have disguised their identities by using a first name only and changing that name. I am grateful to these individuals and to all others who contributed in any way to the writing or publication of this book.

Special thanks to my wife, Barbara, for her support and encouragement, as well as for her patience during the many hours I spent at the computer.